TH**INQ** KINDER GARTEN

Inquiry-based learning in the kindergarten classroom

Authors
Joan Reimer and Deb Watters

THINQ series authors
Jennifer Watt and Jill Colyer

WAVE  LEARNING SOLUTIONS

Published in Canada by Wave Learning Solutions Inc.
617 Logan Ave.
Toronto, ON, Canada, M4K 3C2
email: contact@wavelearningsolutions.com
phone: 1-800-314-4644
website: www.wavelearningsolutions.com

Printed and bound in Canada

2 3 4 – 20 19 18 17

ISBN 978-0-99-500-182-4

Library and Archives Canada Cataloguing in Publication
Reimer, Joan, 1951–, author

   THINQ Kindergarten : inquiry-based learning in the kindergarten classroom / authors: Joan Reimer and Deb Watters.

(THINQ / series authors: Jennifer Watt and Jill Colyer)

ISBN 978-0-9950018-2-4 (softcover)

   1. Inquiry-based learning. 2. Kindergarten. I. Watters, Debbie, 1961-, author II. Title. III. Title: Inquiry-based learning in the kindergarten classroom.

LB1027.23.R45 2017   371.39   C2016-907254-1

Publisher: David Steele
Production editor: Laura Kim
Formatter: Janette Thompson (Jansom)

Contents

Foreword

"*THINQ Kindergarten: Inquiry-based learning in the kindergarten classroom.*" Now this is an exciting book! Are you a parent? I am. Did your newborn learn anything before his or her first day of school? And just how did they learn those thousands of things? I know: As a parent, you prepared meticulous lesson plans each night. No?

Your newborn, like mine, acquired all of that rich learning by simply being curious. We arrive in this world wired to learn. We are sponges. Through your child's earliest inquiries, she quickly discovered that some objects are cold, hard, unresponsive — a table, a chair, the floor. But other objects are warm, soft, they smile or frown, depending on what she does — Mummy, Daddy, siblings. And so learning through inquiry begins — long before the acquisition of language, and long before the ability to walk.

The crucial question for me is: "When your child enters a classroom for the first time, is his experience characterized by ever richer inquiries that stimulate his innate curiosity? Or does that classroom begin to limit, or even stifle his curiosity?"

Teachers who read *THINQ Kindergarten* will acquire the knowledge, skills and strategies to ensure that those first years of school are full of the wonder that children are born with. From the title of the first chapter, "It's all about the wonder," the authors are quick to point out that "inquiry is a stance." It's not a strategy to be pulled out of a long range plan once a week. I would add that inquiry is an attitude. And as such, you the teacher can nurture it in yourself and, in so doing, encourage it in the children with whom you work. The authors ask of the reader, "Are you curious?" If children are

to continue to be curious through their school years, and thereby effective learners, they need curious teachers. So *THINQ Kindergarten* is full of questions: questions for you to ask of your own practice, questions to ask of your colleagues, questions that come from the children themselves, questions that you'll hear from parents. And of course, as in any authentic inquiry, there is never a single, correct answer to any of these questions.

And there is the rub! The authors are keenly aware that for some of us, ambiguity is uncomfortable. That is why many of us have relied for so long upon themed units, typically connected to the calendar — if it's October, it must be a Halloween theme. *THINQ Kindergarten* gently nudges us to loosen up our control over what gets taught, and to begin to "play" (a very important word!) with the idea of listening to children as they constantly wonder "Why...?" "How come ...?" and "What if ...?"

Because at this miraculously formative age, children can and will *tell* you what the content of your curriculum needs to be! Your crucial role is to intentionally guide, facilitate, manage and, most importantly, observe the children in your care.

This introduces the delicate and challenging issue of assessment in the kindergarten context. The authors discuss "pedagogical documentation" in a way that is accessible and full of common sense. Essentially, how do I, the teacher, make the learning in my classroom visible? Visible for children so they learn to become reflective ("metacognitive"); visible for me, the teacher, to help me provide feedback to the child and to adjust instruction; visible for parents so they can see and appreciate their child's growth, areas of continuing need, and how to support the child's learning at home.

THINQ Kindergarten provides a treasure trove of powerful visuals, such as "The stages of documentation," as well as practical observational tools such as "Examples of noticing and naming inquiry learning," which support the teacher in implementing approaches such as pedagogical documentation. There are numerous specific examples of classroom practice presented as "Inquiry in Action" features. Each chapter ends with a built-in study guide that includes three features: the Big Ideas, "Revisit and reflect," and "THINQ" questions to guide the teacher's own inquiry into his or her classroom practice.

In short, *THINQ Kindergarten* is your essential guide to what today's kindergarten program needs to look like. Just "add the children and stir!"

Damian Cooper

Author of *Talk About Assessment: Strategies and Tools to Improve Learning* (2007), *Talk About Assessment: High School Strategies and Tools* (2010), and, *Redefining Fair: How to Plan, Assess, and Grade for Excellence in Mixed-Ability Classrooms* (2011).

Kindergarten authors

photo Joan Reimer

Joan Reimer

Joan is a recently retired educator who began her career as a kindergarten teacher in Ontario. Her former role was Education Officer at the Ontario Ministry of Education. During her career she taught from kindergarten to grade 12 and was an administrator in both the elementary and secondary panels. She also taught courses and supervised student teachers at Brandon University and Arctic College. She has written curriculum materials, prepared courses for principals, and collaborated on ministry documents. Most of her career was spent in Ontario but she also taught in Manitoba, the Northwest Territories and Malawi, Africa.

photo Deb Watters

Deb Watters

Deb has been in education for 28 years. She is currently the Elementary Program Coordinator with the Wellington Catholic District School Board where she wears many hats. She supports new and experienced classroom educators with a particular focus in Collaborative Inquiries, K-8 literacy, English Language Learners, and her passion, Early Learning and Kindergarten. She has taught kindergarten to grade 4 as well as being an Early Literacy Teacher. Deb has taught the Additional Kindergarten Qualifications courses and has presented at a variety of workshops and conferences. She has written and revised curriculum materials for both her board and OECTA. She is also the co-author with her sons of the children's book, *Where's Mom's Hair?: A Family's Journey through Cancer*.

THINQ series authors

photo Jill Colyer

Jill Colyer

Jill is currently the Head of School at Richland Academy. She was recently Director of Teaching and Learning at Bayview Glen Independent School and an Education Officer at the Ontario Ministry of Education. Prior to that, Jill was the National Director of the Historical Thinking Project. Jill was a secondary school teacher and department head with the Waterloo Region District School Board for 15 years. She is a writer of curriculum materials, courses and resources. Her most recent publications are *THINQ 4–6* (2016) and *IQ: A Practical Guide to Inquiry-based Learning*, Oxford University Press (2014).

photo Jennifer Watt

Jennifer Watt

Jennifer is an instructional leader for beginning teachers and their mentors at the Toronto District School Board. She has been a history, politics, social science and English teacher, and a consultant for over 27 years. Throughout her career, she has supported both new and experienced classroom teachers at all grades and subjects in thinking about how to share their knowledge, experience and practices to improve student learning. Jennifer has a Master's Degree focusing on the assessment of teacher practice. She is the author of several books and her most recent publications are *THINQ 4–6* (2016) and *IQ: A Practical Guide to Inquiry-based Learning*, Oxford University Press (2014).

Acknowledgements

It was an honour to learn about inquiry alongside our talented and caring kindergarten educators. Thank you for your conversations and commitment to the learning of our young children.

I am grateful for the collaboration, intelligence and wit of my writing partner Deb, who always challenged my thinking and made me a better person.

My husband, Ab, provided me with the unconditional love that lifted me up and kept me going. Our children Brennan and Kelly, Lindsay and Andrew, Chantelle and Jon, Carolin and Jim, Christine, Dustin and Jen provided ongoing support and encouragement. Our grandchildren Greyson, Reese, Miriam, Maya, Boston and Katie amaze and inspire me with their constant wonders about our world.

Thank you David, Jill and Jennifer for being the visionaries and making inquiry part of our everyday learning in the classroom.

Joan Reimer

A heartfelt thanks to the many kindergarten educators I have had the privilege to co–learn with, especially those who allowed me to share their work and ideas. Your love and commitment to honouring young learners is a true inspiration.

To my colleagues at WCDSB, what a gift it has been to work alongside you all. A special shout out goes to Scott P., who challenged me to ask the question "So what?" I am grateful to David, Jill and Jennifer for facilitating and supporting the creation of this book.

I would like to thank my awesome writing partner Joan with whom I share a common understanding on many things but who also graciously makes me question and wonder. To my family and friends who love and support me unconditionally. To my husband and sons, Shawn, Haydn and Emmett, who fill my life with wonder each and every day.

Deb Watters

Advisory Panel

We would like to thank the following educators who generously read chapters from the book and shared with us their comments and suggestions.

Marianne Bartkiw, Toronto DSB

Jill Bishop, Durham DSB

Margaret DaSilva, Toronto DSB

Carmelina DiGrigoli, York Region DSB

Becky Kennedy, Simcoe County DSB

About THINQ

Making inquiry-based learning a practical reality for every classroom!

An ever increasing number of educators are exploring the potential of inquiry-based pedagogies to build a bridge to teaching, learning and assessment in a digital age. They instinctively understand that asking questions and seeking answers is a natural way of being a learner in the world. However, translating this basic truth into daily instructional practice is no small thing. This is the focus of *THINQ* — to help make inquiry-based learning a practical reality for every classroom, teacher and student.

We are writing the *THINQ* professional learning series from a teacher perspective, with an empathetic and realistic appreciation of a teacher's daily challenges. *THINQ* is designed to help teachers see how, over time, they can realistically integrate more inquiry-based learning into the context of their own classrooms.

THINQ resources are designed to:

- encourage teachers to do more inquiry.
- explore the big ideas of inquiry in an accessible and reader-friendly way.
- make explicit what inquiry can look, feel and sound like.
- demonstrate how inquiry-based learning can be assessed and evaluated.
- pose deep questions for teacher self-reflection and discussion with colleagues.
- provide case studies that introduce practical strategies with contextual examples.
- address common teacher questions and misconceptions about inquiry.

THINQ emphasizes the big ideas that underpin inquiry-based learning regardless of grades and disciplines. We also apply them to the specific needs and characteristics of learners at different ages and developmental stages: *THINQ Kindergarten*, *THINQ 1–3* (Primary), *THINQ 4–6* (Junior) and *THINQ 7–9* (Intermediate). We recognize that school jurisdictions organize their schools and grade divisions differently, but all of us share the understanding that there are distinct developmental learning stages. So while "junior learner" may not be the designation for grades 4–6 in your system, we feel confident, based on our work with teachers, that the students, issues and challenges are the same.

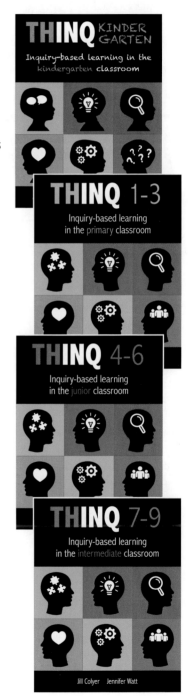

Professional learning — a personal journey

We believe that transforming the daily assessment and instructional practice of teachers is the single most important consideration in transitioning the traditional education system to digital-age teaching and learning models. But because change is hard, it is only really achievable if and when educators, individually and in collaborative communities, believe passionately in its benefits. They must choose voluntarily (not through coercion or compliance) to take up the challenge to change classroom practice and school culture. This is what *THINQ* is all about — helping educators reflect upon and move forward along their individual professional learning path.

We believe that integrating more inquiry rests, in part, upon a deep **conviction** that inquiry-based learning is needed and a personal **commitment** to persist until classrooms and schools begin to operate differently. Building the **capacity** to implement more inquiry in the **context** of one's own classroom and school is only sustainable if positive outcomes are **confirmed** by evidence and shared with others. Margin prompts throughout this book use these five Cs to provoke reflection, individually or with your colleagues, about your journey into inquiry-based learning.

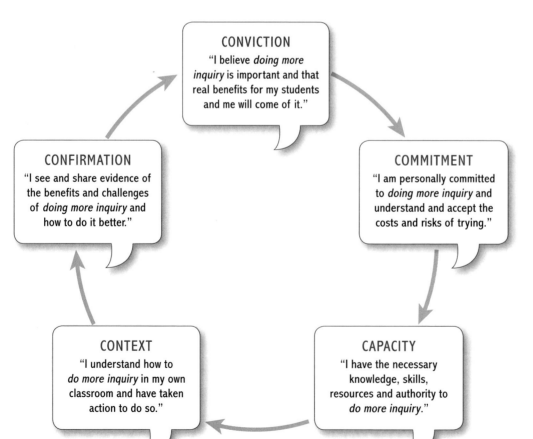

CONVICTION
"I believe *doing more inquiry* is important and that real benefits for my students and me will come of it."

COMMITMENT
"I am personally committed to *doing more inquiry* and understand and accept the costs and risks of trying."

CAPACITY
"I have the necessary knowledge, skills, resources and authority to *do more inquiry*."

CONTEXT
"I understand how to *do more inquiry* in my own classroom and have taken action to do so."

CONFIRMATION
"I see and share evidence of the benefits and challenges of *doing more inquiry* and how to do it better."

THINQ

- How well do these statements reflect where you and your colleagues are currently?

- What is the relationship between the Five Cs?

- How can you use the Five Cs to assess progress on your professional quest to do more inquiry?

Chapter 1

IT'S ALL ABOUT
THE WONDER:
Inquiry-based learning
in kindergarten

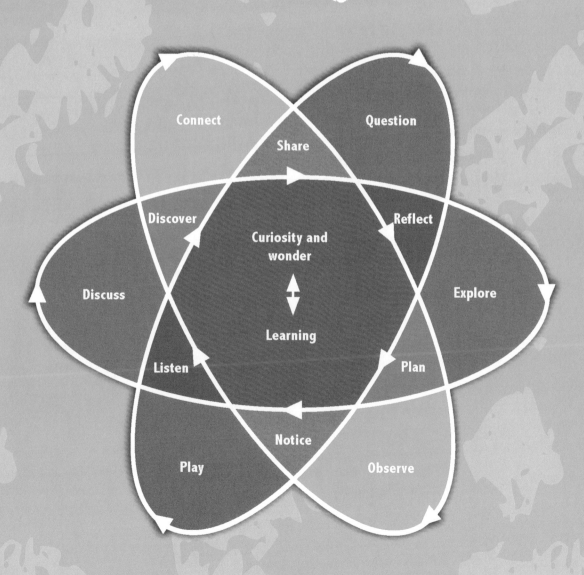

1.1 What is inquiry learning?

Inquiry learning is anchored in our curiosity and innate desire to make sense of the world around us. When we ask questions, have wonderings, and use our heads and our hearts to investigate what fascinates us and confounds our thinking, we are engaged in inquiry. Inquiry is a dynamic process that builds on the wonderings of both children and educators. Thus, inquiry is more than a process of learning. It is a way of being as a learner; it is a stance.

But what does it actually mean and look like to take an inquiry stance to teaching and learning? It involves co-creating and establishing a culture that supports living in an inquiry stance within the classroom and the school. A culture of inquiry allows all learners, adults and children alike, to explore wonderings, ideas and questions. Inquiry-based learning supports students' questions and ideas, not just the educator's, as the basis of learning experiences.

Inquiry learning has been around as long as educators have encouraged and supported intellectual curiosity. Inquiry poses an alternative to rote learning. It is a form of deep thinking that allows children to learn how to learn, as opposed to having what to learn decided for them, most often in the form of isolated and decontextualized content.

Inquiry offers opportunities for children to develop metacognitive skills, think about their learning, and make meaningful connections to knowledge and skills. As educators, we are called on not only to shed light on our learners' experiences, but on the thinking and learning that is happening throughout the journey. Inquiry is neither subject-specific nor relegated to a certain time of day, but is embedded in all learning.

THINQ

- How infused with the spirit of inquiry is your classroom?
- How do the quotes of Rinaldi and Pacini-Ketchabaw resonate with you as an educator and a learner?

Food for Thought

"We don't have to teach them to ask 'why?' because inside each human being is the need to understand the reasons, the meaning of the world around us and the meaning of our life."

Carla Rinaldi

"The role of the educator shifts from a communicator of knowledge to a listener, provocateur, documenter, and negotiator of meaning."

Veronica Pacini-Ketchabaw

Curiosity and wonder

FIGURE 1.1 Children and educators in an inquiry stance means curiosity and wonder infuses all their teaching and learning.

The spirit of inquiry

Cara and Amanda set out a tub full of coloured corn and gourds as a provocation. The children started scraping and picking the corn off the cob. Corn kernels were flying and falling all over the floor. It was becoming an unsafe situation for the learners. Cara and Amanda called the children together to pose the question about how they could play with the corn and still be safe. A number of the children said they would gladly sweep up the kernels so that no one would slip and fall. They also discussed how the popping kernels were unsafe for everyone's eyes. One of the learners suggested safely glasses, as she had seen her dad using them before. The next day a number of the children brought in safety glasses, as did the educators.

Once all the corn had been taken off the cobs, Cara posed the question, "I wonder what we can do with all this loose corn?" The learners suggested using the corn to feed animals. Then the educators asked, "What can be done with the cobs?" The next day a number of artists took the corn cobs to the paint center and painted coloured patterns on the cobs.

The educators then posed the question "What could be done with the painted cobs?" The learners put the cobs in a basket and used them as manipulatives for many different experiences.

This is a wonderful example of educators who are in an inquiry stance. When things became messy and possibly unsafe, they negotiated a solution with the learners. They also let the children take the lead with the materials by posing the questions "What will we do next?" The initial provocation of the corn cobs grew into a multilayered inquiry because of the educators' stance, their willingness to deal with not knowing what might come next, the posing of open-ended questions, and their understanding that children are co-creators of inquiry and next steps.

> ### Conviction
> How convinced are you that the optimal conditions for learning involve an educator adopting an inquiry stance?

FIGURE 1.2 What would your learners do with all that messy corn?

1.2 How can we support inquiry dispositions in kindergarten?

Big Idea
Educators must cultivate and respect the natural inquiry dispositions in every child.

Children are naturally full of questions, have active imaginations and are motivated to understand the world in which they live. Educators are called on to cultivate and respect these dispositions that are in every child. We should spend significant time creating an inquiry culture that supports both the affective and cognitive elements of inquiry.

In supporting inquiry dispositions, educators co-create meaningful, authentic learning and experiences that lead to deep understanding. As educators, we encourage our students when they think and reflect on their learning; we too must be reflective about our professional learning and practice. Being in an inquiry stance, as opposed to "doing" an inquiry, opens educators to ongoing inquiry of our practice and reflection on learning.

Conviction
How convinced are you that curiosity, reflection, resiliency and open-mindedness are necessary conditions for learning in kindergarten?

Inquiry dispositions

Curiosity, open-mindedness, reflection and resiliency in your ability to learn and reason are inquiry dispositions — or what some call "inquiry habits of mind." They are what keeps the learner on the journey of inquiry. These dispositions support risk-taking and commitment to inquiry learning. They make us perseverant and more able to accept failure and mistakes as an important part of the journey.

Capacity
What do you think you need to learn in order to further engage yourself and your learners in meaningful inquiry-based learning?

Curiosity	**Reflection**	**Resiliency**	**Open-mindedness**
Eagerness to learn or know something	Ability to think about thinking	Capacity to keep on trying and overcome	Willingness to consider new ideas

FIGURE 1.3 Curiosity, reflection, resiliency and open-mindedness are essential building blocks for creating a sustainable culture of inquiry-based learning.

Co-learning and co-creation

Inquiry-based learning challenges us to be co-learners and co-investigators with our students. A co-learning relationship is established when children and educators pursue significant questions about authentic and relevant ideas together. When we talk with kindergarten educators who are engaged in inquiry learning, we see that they are learning alongside their students and are excited by the prospect of doing so. They are passionate and curious about their world, critical and creative thought, and their own teaching. Throughout this book we look at how educators can be co-learners and creators.

Patterns of dialogue

When educators listen, observe and ask questions about the interests of young children, children feel valued. Through this manner of inquiry, educators demonstrate that they believe that children are proficient, talented and intelligent. When educators have an inquiry stance, they rethink the patterns of dialogue that are happening in their learning environment in order to support the dispositions of inquiry. We are attempting to move from "knowledge telling" to a community that supports "knowledge building." The traditional patterns of dialogue in a classroom have often focused on the educators doing the talking — but those that do the talking are often doing the learning. To support inquiry dispositions, there needs to be a shift in the pattern of dialogue. Communication should be encouraged to happen amongst all learners. When everyone shares ideas, wonderings and discoveries, learning dispositions thrive and expand.

FIGURE 1.4 Children need to see and hear educators as thinkers and learners, engaging in wondering, planning, investigating, creating and rethinking.

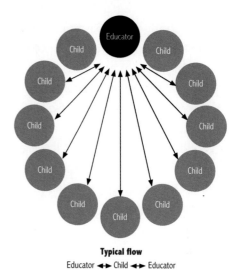

Typical flow
Educator ◄►► Child ◄►► Educator

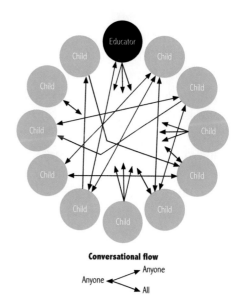

Conversational flow
Anyone ◄—— Anyone
Anyone ——► All

FIGURE 1.5 Traditional patterns of dialogue involve educators doing most of the talking and "knowledge telling." But to foster inquiry dispositions, communication patterns need to shift the classroom environment towards "knowledge building." Source: Lewin-Benham, *Twelve Best Practices of Early Childhood Education*.

Provocation

Our job is to help young learners see the world — to notice and explore what is interesting, amusing, different, confusing, conflicting and contradictory. When we rethink our role as being provocateurs rather than just facilitators, we come to understand that facilitators simplify and expedite experiences, while provocateurs provoke, point out dissonance and generate additional questions to further learning. These actions nurture the natural inquiry dispositions that young learners have. Provocations can begin in many ways and we'll look more closely at this in Chapter 2.

Authenticity

To nurture and grow inquiry dispositions, learning experiences must be authentic. Authenticity derives from the genuine wonder and curiosity of learners. Learning begins with questions and problems that are real, important and essential for learners. Authenticity also means honest reflection, sharing, and the candid admission, especially by educators to children, of the possibility of difficulty or challenges during an inquiry.

Tolerance for ambiguity

Inquiry educators also talk about overcoming their own fear and trepidation when conducting inquiry, which comes from never knowing for sure what may happen. This initial fear changes to excitement as they see the benefits to student learning and engagement. These educators have tried and stumbled and tried again to create and hone strategies to make their students better inquiry learners.

Words Matter

Provocation
A deliberate action or occurrence that causes someone to begin to do something.

Capacity
What is your tolerance for the uncertainty and ambiguity of inquiry?

Educators Ask

Am I already doing inquiry-based learning?

Educators frequently wonder: "Am I doing inquiry?" If you are engaging children in asking their own questions, exploring their wonderings, asking them open-ended questions, provoking their curiosity, and supporting them to think deeply about their own learning and the world around them, then you are "doing inquiry."

So typically the issue is not if we are "doing inquiry," but determining:

- "How can we offer more opportunities for inquiry in our classrooms?"
- "How can we deepen opportunities for thinking throughout an inquiry?"
- "How can we foster inquiry dispositions through all aspects of learning?
- "How can we gather evidence of learning during inquiry?"

That's where this book comes in. We hope to offer practical examples to deepen and support you and your students' inquiry-based learning journey.

Beliefs about learners

Perhaps more than anything else, sustaining and nurturing inquiry dispositions must be deeply rooted in positive beliefs about the potential of all learners — that they are "competent, capable of complex thinking, curious and rich in potential" (*How Does Learning Happen*).

Inquiry-based learning encourages human curiosity. It demands rigorous thought. It involves knowledge building and it pushes the learner to repeatedly explore ideas from new perspectives and viewpoints. Learners are in control and are active, rather than passive, participants in the learning process.

Therefore, successful inquiry educators have confidence in their students' abilities and are responsive to their interests. These educators take appropriate risks in their teaching by following the curiosity of their students and by challenging them to question, explore and conclude, and to stretch beyond the obvious and easy-to-answer questions.

THINQ

- Would you add any other ways to nurture inquiry dispositions beyond than the ones described here?
- Which ones do you think would yield the best results in the context of your own classroom?
- What are your beliefs about the learners in your classroom?
- Which of the reflective questions could you answer most positively and which ones were more challenging?

Inquiry in Action

Reflective questions for kindergarten educators

An inquiry stance to learning means being reflective of one's own practice. How would you answer the following questions?

- Am I curious?
- Do I think out loud about my wonderings?
- Am I a co-learner?
- Am I flexible and spontaneous?
- Am I willing to yield the plan I currently have for an opportunity that arises in the moment?
- Am I open to act on opportunities for learning?
- Do I offer multiple ways for students to demonstrate skills and knowledge?
- Do I provide materials and resources that allow for inquiries to grow?
- Do I reflect on student wonderings and use these as next steps?
- Do I engage learners in frequent discussions about learning?
- Have I created a safe environment that allows children to take risks?
- Do I know and focus on big ideas and conceptual understandings?
- Do I support and encourage students to investigate their wonderings?

1.3 What does the inquiry process look like in kindergarten?

Big Idea
Inquiry is a non-linear process.

We are aware that most children (and adults for that matter) do not move through the learning process in a linear or lockstep way. They may move one step forward and then two steps back; they may enter in and then retreat; and they may jump over, skip or bounce around. It depends on the situation; their disposition at the time; the content, topic, or problem under investigation; their developmental level; their motivation; and their experience with inquiry-based learning. It has been a challenge for us to come up with an inquiry-process model graphic that accurately reflects this non-linear reality.

Food for Thought

"There is no definitive endpoint to the learning process. Students continually formulate and reformulate their ideas and theories with each added layer of lived experience."

Natural Curiosity

Inquiry model

Having said that, we feel that Figure 1.6 is a useful way to visualize inquiry-based learning. Curiosity and wonder are the anchor in the middle, setting thinking in motion. The learning that follows is responsive to the individual and is iterative and flexible, with lots of looping back and reconsidering as knowledge builds. As understanding develops, more questions arise, rethinking occurs and learning becomes deeper. Communication is ongoing when educators and learners share and reflect as they question, explore and solve.

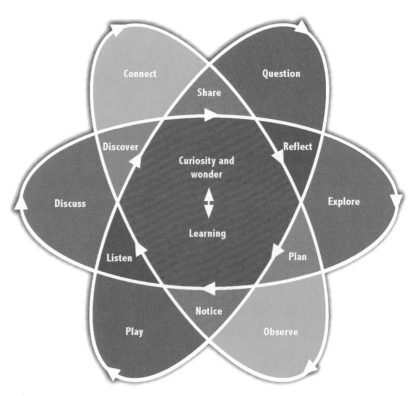

FIGURE 1.6 This model is intended to represent the fluid, ongoing, recursive, iterative and non-linear nature of inquiry.

It is difficult to see this process as linear since as understanding is being developed, more questions arise, rethinking occurs, and learners need to go deeper, setting the actions in motion again. The dissonance created by the questioning nature of inquiry is what keeps the process fluid and learners thinking.

Inquiry thinking

Ron Richart describes actions that are made when thinking and understanding transpire. These actions are intrinsic to inquiry and would flow through the inquiry model not in any particular order, but naturally. These skills transcend content mastery and are lifelong competencies.

Traits of inquiry

The term "inquiry" can be an elusive one, since inquiry learning shares important characteristics and traits with other pedagogies such as active learning, discovery learning and problem-based learning. Your grade division, school or school district may be trying out various forms of inquiry learning, or may be a proponent of one or two. To simplify this, all of these pedagogies share a common purpose, which is to make a child an effective and independent learner by giving him or her opportunities to build knowledge. We find it helpful to grasp the three essential traits as described in Figure 1.8.

THINQ

- How does our description of inquiry in kindergarten resonate with you and what you know and understand about inquiry? Is there anything you would add or modify?

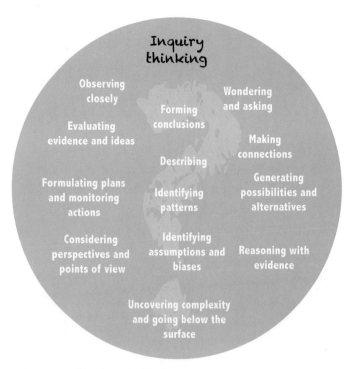

FIGURE 1.7 Ron Richart describes the thinking that is intrinsic to inquiry. Source: *Making Thinking Visible.*

available online

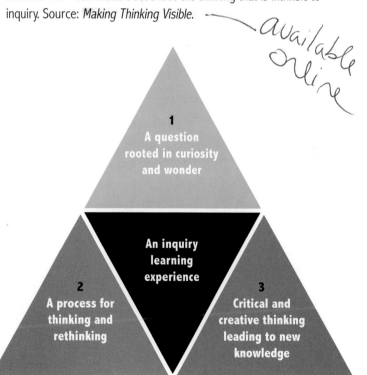

FIGURE 1.8 All inquiry experiences share three common traits.

1.4 How does inquiry differ from a traditional kindergarten program?

Big Idea

Inquiry classrooms focus on big ideas, key concepts and transferrble skills

Inquiry-based learning gives children opportunities to build knowledge and fosters effective and independent learners. Children learn best when they are fully invested in the process of knowledge building, rather than the educator deciding when and how knowledge will be dispersed.

We are moving away from seeing educators as all-knowing authority figures to seeing them as conceptual thinkers and co-learners who are skilled at asking questions that provoke wonder in their students. This encourages us to ask ourselves if the experiences we are offering support knowledge and skill creation that are built and shared based on student interest and need, rather than themes or seasonal activities.

Food for Thought

"With the learner at the centre … Our role as teachers shifts from the delivery of information to fostering student's engagement with ideas. Instead of covering the curriculum and judging our success by how much content we get through, we engage, struggle, question, explore and ultimately build understanding."

Ron Richart

The knowledge and skills of inquiry in kindergarten are reflected in the conceptual understandings, big ideas, and overall and specific expectations. We are taking a journey with our students as we rethink our focus from the completion of work and activities towards making thinking and learning visible for all, and co-developing an inquiry stance. As educators, we need to continually ask ourselves if we are providing our students with activities and rote learning, or cultivating thinking and inquiry. Intentional guidance can be required as knowledge building is occurring.

Traditional teaching	Inquiry teaching
Educator is the expert	Educator is a **co-learner**
Educator tells	Educator **models**
Educator controls	Educator **activates**
Educator corrects mistakes	Educator **gives feedback**
Educator gives answers	Educator **asks questions**
Educator is a manager	Educator is a **provocateur**
Educator assesses task completion	Educator **assesses learning**

FIGURE 1.9 In an inquiry-based classroom, students benefit when educators participate as co-learners who model and activate learning.

We know that children learn best when they are fully invested in the process of knowledge building, rather than when educators alone decide when and how knowledge will be dispersed. Therefore, we need to ask ourselves whether the experiences we are offering support knowledge creation and skill building — built and shared based on student interest and need — rather than the exploration of a teacher selected theme or seasonal activity.

Early educators traditionally organized the learning in their classrooms around themes, e.g., September is "Back to School," October is "Autumn." While this satisfies our need to be planned and organized for the year, it may inadvertently preclude rich learning opportunities in our classrooms. Consider Figure 1.10 on the next page, which outlines the differences between a traditional kindergarten program and an inquiry-based approach.

This table illustrates that an inquiry-based kindergarten classroom is focused on the learning of concepts, big ideas and transferable skills, as opposed to the coverage of predetermined content or the completion of tasks. This means that kindergarten children will acquire knowledge through the inquiry process itself (we will look more closely at this in Chapter 4). A kindergarten program that is inquiry-based will also foster effective and independent learners.

One of the limitations of themes or seasonal celebrations is that students are not given time after an experience to consolidate the new knowledge they have gained. Children learn through play experiences by communicating about them and representing their learning in multiple ways. Inquiry-based learning allows children to revisit concepts, new ideas and consolidate their learning, and it gives educators opportunities to notice and name the learning.

THINQ

- In what ways does the quote by Ron Richart resonate with your understanding of an educator's role in an inquiry-based classroom?

- How is your classroom environment more theme-based or inquiry-based?

- When you reflect on the Halloween vignette, how do you manage the dissonance about being guided by student interest versus thematic content and community expectations?

Conviction

How convinced are you that child-driven inquiry offers richer learning opportunities than a more educator-directed program?

Inquiry in Action

Rethinking themes

Let's consider a snapshot of Jean-Paul and Kate's classroom with the question "How might themes preclude rich learning opportunities?" in mind.

Right after Halloween, the students decided that they wanted to set up a haunted house at the drama centre. Jean-Paul and Kate were reluctant because Halloween was over and Halloween was not part of November's planning.

Eventually they agreed to let the students proceed. The children co-created a haunted house with spooky ghosts, bats and skeletons.

Throughout the construction of the haunted house, the educators observed the learners discussing the experiences they had leading up to Halloween night, what it was like to go out for Halloween and what was it like to be scared. In this case, the learners were revisiting their experience and making their learning and new wonderings visible.

Comparing a traditional program with an inquiry-based approach

Elements	Traditional	Inquiry-based
Duration	Length of the learning experience is fixed and predetermined.	Length of the learning experience is determined by the inquiry progression.
Topics	Determined by educator and curriculum, and may or may not be of interest to students.	Negotiated by educator and student, with integrated curriculum goals; students' interest is the inquiry focus.
Planning	Educator plans topics and designs learning experiences in advance.	Educator listens to student wonderings, observes children and uses student interest to determine the next steps.
Objectives	Educator decides based on curriculum goals and may or may not include inquiry experiences.	Educator assesses students' prior knowledge to determine where inquiry and learning could go next.
Knowledge building	Knowledge is gained through educator-designed experiences, activities and events.	Knowledge is gained through exploration, investigation and communication in flexible groupings.
Resources	Resources are provided by the educator.	Resources are brought in by students, educators and experts.
Time	Topics are often taught at specific educator-determined times of day and in specific spaces.	Inquiry permeates the day and the environment, involving many different curriculum areas and skills.
Focus	Activities are planned by the educator to focus on specific concepts.	Learning focuses on exploration, investigation and communication. Educator notices and names the learning.
Assessment	Typically of products of completed tasks from predetermined activities.	Includes a balance of observations, conversations and products generated through the inquiry.
Evidence of learning	Usually one method of representation selected by the educator (e.g., paper and pencil).	Children demonstrate learning in a meaningful manner (e.g., drawing, writing, building, constructing, videoing, drama and dance).

FIGURE 1.10 There are significant differences between a traditional kindergarten program and an inquiry-based approach.

1.5 How does inquiry in kindergarten support integrated learning?

Big Idea

Inquiry-based learning supports the integration of different subjects and disciplines.

An effective inquiry-based kindergarten program supports an integrated learning model as opposed to teaching only by discipline or subject. Students are innately curious and make natural connections among disciplines. Learning in an integrated way honours the child and their individual learning styles, interests, strengths and ability to grow.

By validating these elements, we guide our learners towards a stronger sense of identity and purpose. It is our role as educators to create the environment that supports the curiosity and to then notice and name these connections to make the learning visible.

Confirmation

If you have used an integrated learning model in your classroom, what successes and challenges did you have?

Inquiry opens up the possibility of seeing all disciplines made observable in an authentic way. While an inquiry-based approach makes integrated learning easier to plan and implement, educators still need intimate knowledge and deep understanding of the overarching curriculum goals and the developmental stages of their students so that connections can be noticed and named throughout a more open-ended inquiry process.

In an integrated, inquiry-driven classroom, explicit teaching of skills and knowledge is still an important component of a kindergarten program. However, it is done in an authentic context, based on the interests, curiosity and wonderings of children. Therefore, inquiry-based learning provides genuine reasons to use and develop skills such as reading and writing in ways that blur the traditional separation of discrete subject areas.

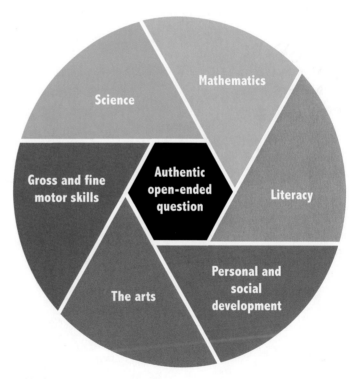

FIGURE 1.11 Inquiry-based learning, by its very nature, is integrated and multi-disciplinary.

Subject integration during observations and conversations about plants

Antonella placed a summer planter with a variety of plants in the classroom as a provocation. She and her teaching partner Laurie observed and documented the students' conversations about the planter. The children's conversation turned towards whether the plants in the planter would survive or not. They discussed which plants in the planters would survive and which had no hope. A tally chart that reflected the children's predictions was co-created.

A: "The tall leaves will die."
K: "The purple flowers will live."
D: "I think the geraniums will bloom."

During the inquiry, the learners observed and recorded their observations, and the educators documented the learning. They theorized what plants needed to live, such as soil, water, sun … and love! The children kept a really close eye on the plants and decided to write messages of hope to the plants so that they would keep on growing.

- YOUR R THE BEST PLANT EVR."
- I LOVE U"
- I THINK U BUTIFUL."

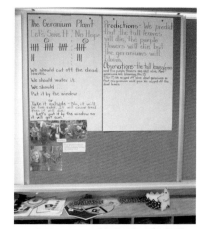

FIGURE 1.12 Antonella documented and made the learning visible.

FIGURE 1.13 This kindergarten inquiry illustrates that many disciplines can be explored and uncovered through inquiry. The role of the educator is to notice and name the learning.

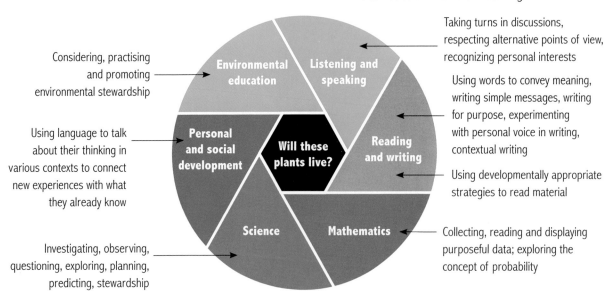

Considering, practising and promoting environmental stewardship

Using language to talk about their thinking in various contexts to connect new experiences with what they already know

Investigating, observing, questioning, exploring, planning, predicting, stewardship

Environmental education

Personal and social development

Will these plants live?

Science

Listening and speaking

Reading and writing

Mathematics

Taking turns in discussions, respecting alternative points of view, recognizing personal interests

Using words to convey meaning, writing simple messages, writing for purpose, experimenting with personal voice in writing, contextual writing

Using developmentally appropriate strategies to read material

Collecting, reading and displaying purposeful data; exploring the concept of probability

1.6 What is the relationship between play-based and inquiry-based learning?

Play is the foundation

Play is the way that children learn about themselves and their world. Inquiry is one approach to teaching and learning, or pedagogy within the foundational context of play. Other pedagogies include self-directed learning, cooperative learning, guided discovery, problem-based learning, and project-based learning. Many of the skills and dispositions of inquiry are inherent in play. Educators use their prior knowledge and understanding to make sense of their children's play. Educators use their knowledge of conceptual understandings, program expectations and their learners to reflect on new thinking and formulate next steps through negotiation with children.

For young children, inquiry through play is instinctive. Active, self-initiated experiences are the foundation of this natural instinct and support the development of inquiry dispositions such as curiosity, reflection, resiliency and open-mindedness. Play allows children to engage in inquiry with others; initiate interactions; exchange ideas, materials, and points of view; and resolve conflicts in social problem-solving situations.

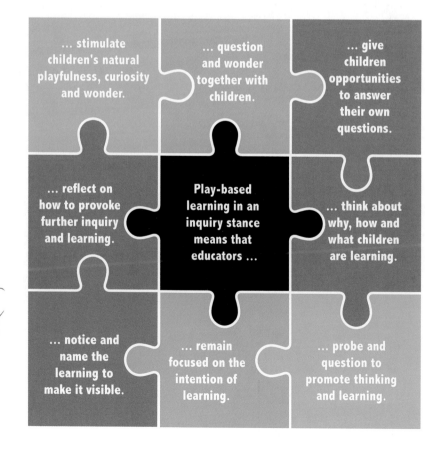

... stimulate children's natural playfulness, curiosity and wonder.

... question and wonder together with children.

... give children opportunities to answer their own questions.

... reflect on how to provoke further inquiry and learning.

Play-based learning in an inquiry stance means that educators ...

... think about why, how and what children are learning.

... notice and name the learning to make it visible.

... remain focused on the intention of learning.

... probe and question to promote thinking and learning.

FIGURE 1.14 Play is a "vehicle for learning" and an educator's role is to promote, identify and extend children's learning along the way.

The importance of play

Play serves many purposes. It supports the physical, intellectual, emotional, social and moral development of young children. Participants in play direct their own actions, making it an expression of free will and an assertion of liberty. Play is an interest or pastime for its own sake. It is more about the process than the product and there may not be an end goal. When there are goals in play, they are secondary to the means.

Play allows for and fosters creativity and learning because the player feels free to experiment. Through play, children are active contributors and learn to regulate themselves, their actions and their mental selves. These conditions are ideal for the learning of new skills and is why play is seen as an important component of all kindergarten programs.

The importance of play goes beyond the walls of our classrooms. Play is so significant that the United Nations has recognized it as a right for all children in all parts of the world. Article 31 of the United Nations Convention on the Rights of the Child states that: "States parties recognize the right of the child to rest and leisure, to engage in play and recreational activities appropriate to the age of the child and to participate freely in cultural life and the arts." It is an approach to everyday living everywhere for all youth.

If you need to share the importance and value of play-based learning with colleagues and parents, you may find Reproducible 1A, *CMEC statement on play-based learning* helpful.

THINQ

- Why do you think play is not always considered to be a form of learning?

- How is play viewed in your school or district: as something to be tightly-controlled, or fostered and integrated into the entire day?

- Are you clear about the relationship between play and inquiry? What else would you like to know?

FIGURE 1.15 Reproducible 1A, p. RE1.

1.7 Is inquiry appropriate for kindergarten learners?

Inquiry involves the most natural ways young children learn at early stages of cognitive development. They can ask questions, seek answers and share their discoveries. Early learning is the foundation for inquiry at a later level when students can think more abstractly.

Young learners are developing the skills and knowledge that inquiry-based learning allows them to practice. An inquiry-based environment also allows children to be self-directed, learn through their interests, demonstrate knowledge in multiple ways, exercise choice and use their voice. It supports the child's capacity to develop self-regulatory behaviour, which includes responding to stressful situations and being able to deal with new challenges.

Through purposeful inquiry-based learning, students practice and develop conceptual understandings and skills in all areas. The integrated nature of inquiry enhances social, mental and physical well-being for kindergarten learners. Inquiry allows for the development of new learning in many realms.

Big Idea

Kindergarten learners have emerging qualities that can be intentionally strengthened through inquiry.

Food for Thought

"Neither inquiry nor the taking on of a critical perspective is something for the later years. It needs to happen from the very start."

Jerome Harste

FIGURE 1.16 Inquiry supports the emerging qualities and dispositions of kindergarten learners. Adapted from ELECT.

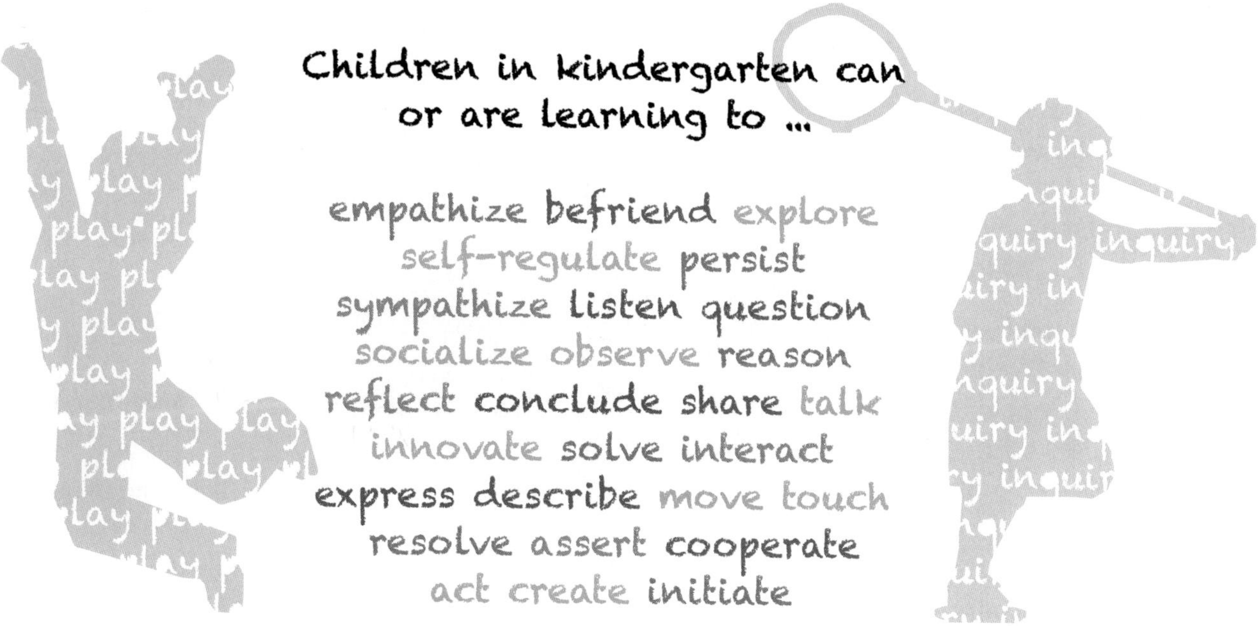

Children in kindergarten can or are learning to ...

empathize befriend explore
self-regulate persist
sympathize listen question
socialize observe reason
reflect conclude share talk
innovate solve interact
express describe move touch
resolve assert cooperate
act create initiate

1.8 Is inquiry a better way to learn?

As educators, we may intuitively feel that inquiry-based learning is a better, and more natural way for children to learn. But are our assumptions supported by research? In short, yes. Absolutely!

Foundational research

Inquiry learning is rooted in progressive and constructivist educational philosophies of the early 19th century. Progressive educators, such as John Dewey, proposed that learners should "do" the discipline by thinking, communicating and verifying knowledge in an authentic manner. He felt that passive, transmission-based pedagogies were flawed since the memorization of facts, discrete procedures and algorithms were quickly forgotten because the learner had no part in working with them or in building new knowledge that was relevant to them or to the real world.

The bases of a social constructivist theory were laid by Vygotsky, who stressed the fundamental role of social interaction in the development of cognition. He emphasized the collaborative nature of learning, the importance of cultural and social context, and that learning is an active, ongoing process that continues throughout life.

Paulo Freire advocated for an education where learners would critically engage with knowledge by grappling and building upon what is known, and strive to change the world based on creating new knowledge.

Loris Malaguzzi was the driving force behind the world-renowned approach to education embodied in the Reggio Emilia early childhood schools of Italy, first established after World War II. Malaguzzi believed that children should be viewed as competent, capable individuals that deserved to be treated with respect. He also believed that children learn naturally through inquiry and play, and that it is our job as educators to foster the wonder of learning.

Food for Thought

"The wider the range of possibilities we offer children, the more intense their motivations and the richer their experiences."

Loris Malaguzzi

Traditional learning	Inquiry learning
Have to learn	Want to learn
What to know	How to know
Tell and memorize	Ask and inquire
Only one right answer	Many conclusions
Teacher-directed	Learner-centred
One-size-fits-all	Personalized
Passive learning	Active learning
Assess for marks	Assess for learning

FIGURE 1.17 By taking an inquiry stance, many important aspects of best practice teaching, learning and assessment can be advanced.

Contemporary thinking about inquiry

While the foundational thinking around inquiry goes back many decades, contemporary educational researchers and thinkers like the ones below continue to advocate passionately for the relevance and necessity of pursuing an inquiry approach to teaching and learning in a digital age.

Timperley, Kaser and Halbert, Spiral of Inquiry (2014)
"We think that a key requirement for young people today is the development of curiosity. ... [W]e want our learners to leave our settings each year more curious than when they started. We believe this is much more likely to happen if young people are learning in highly engaging and innovative settings where curiosity — for everyone — is a way of life."

Wien, Emergent Curriculum in the Primary Classroom (2008)
"If we permit children and teachers to engage with their own questions, their own theories about how things work, and their own processes for making things happen and understanding the world, then we can guarantee interest and motivation. Motivation fuels learning; it is the positive energy that carries the learner through the curriculum."

Kuhlithau, Maniotes, Caspari, Guided Inquiry in the 21st Century (2007)
"Inquiry... requires more than simply answering questions or getting a right answer. It espouses investigation, exploration, search, quest, research, pursuit and study. It is enhanced by involvement with a community of learners, each learning from the other in social interaction."

"An inquiry approach to teaching and learning seeks to develop independent academic competency, career readiness, and life skills, essential in all schools for all students."

Rinaldi, The Relationship Between Documentation and Assessment (2004)
"In this attitude to find answers to questions are the roots of philosophy. This why is the only way in which to maintain what is essential in our life ... curiosity. Humanity exists because we have developed our curiosity. In the search for reasons and information lie the roots of ethics."

Conviction

How convinced are you that research provides evidence of the benefits of inquiry-based learning? What else would you like to know?

Confirmation

How do your own classroom experiences confirm or contradict the experts?

Educators Ask

Isn't all learning inquiry?

Learning is a broad term that includes any gaining of new knowledge or skill. We learn through experience, practise, study and other means. Inquiry is born out of curiosity. It always begins with a wondering — a problem, a challenge, a question.

Revisit and reflect

This introductory chapter explored the possibilities of inquiry learning in kindergarten classrooms, including what it is, how it benefits the learner and what it means to take an inquiry stance to learning. We looked at nurturing inquiry dispositions and at the relationship between inquiry-based learning and other current aspects of kindergarten teaching and learning, such as themes, subject integration and play-based learning. Finally, we discussed the capacity of early learners to engage in inquiry and how inquiry strengthens their emerging qualities and skills.

THINQ

- What are the opportunities and challenges you face in "going deeper" with inquiry learning?

- Which inquiry dispositions do your students possess? How might you support the growth of inquiry dispositions for your students?

- Consider Reproducible 1B, *Teacher inquiry readiness checklist.* How ready are you?

- With your colleagues, consider Reproducible 1C, *The inquiry process.* How does this compare to your current practice and capacity for inquiry?

- Is there anyone with whom would like to share or discuss Reproducible 1D, *8 big ideas about inquiry-based learning in kindergarten?*

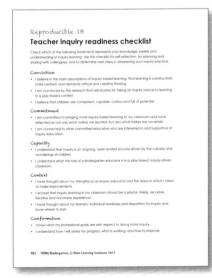

FIGURE 1.18 Reproducible 1B, p. RE2.

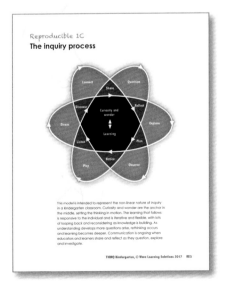

FIGURE 1.19 Reproducible 1C, p. RE3.

FIGURE 1.20 Reproducible 1D, p. RE4.

Chapter 2
WONDERING AND QUESTIONING:
The key to inquiry learning

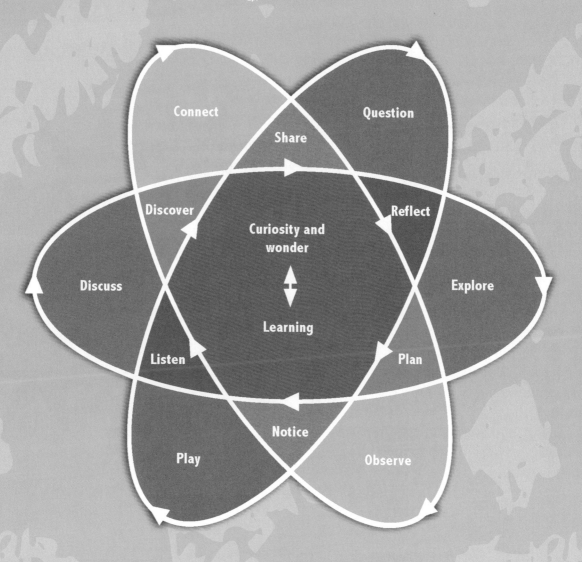

2.1 How can I nurture wonder in my classroom?

Big Idea
Curiosity activates learning.

We believe that young children have an innate sense of curiosity and wonder. It is this curiosity that sparks inquiry, questioning and the need to know. It is from questioning that learning begins and knowledge is constructed.

Putting learner's questions at the centre of classrooms is mandatory for nurturing wonder. A program driven by questions may cause uncertainty and hesitance on the part of the educator, but this is in keeping with the inquiry stance. It is not meant to be easy, as all learners are challenged, including the educator.

Educators can intentionally spark questions with provocations, materials and shared learning experiences. They can also be open to the questions that learners are posing spontaneously. This implies having an open mind, being in an inquiry stance and most importantly, being a good listener. We have found that many rich inquiries have come from queries and interests that students have shared directly with educators, or that educators have overheard, documented and followed up on.

Looking for answers and

Authentic inquiry is launched with questions or problems that learners want answers to *Wanting to know more about something* or want to find out more about. There is a common misunderstanding that educators must wait for the right question for an inquiry to start. Anything that sparks students' interest can be the right question. There are times when questions may not lead to deep inquiries, or there may be provocations that we think will spark an engaging investigation but don't. Don't be discouraged! Questions, shared events or conflicts will arise and meaningful inquiry will happen. Don't wait for it — be engaged, maintain an inquiry stance and develop a pedagogy of listening, and your learners will lead you there.

Food for Thought

"The important thing is not to stop questioning. Curiosity has its own reason for existing."
Albert Einstein

"We are extremely good question-asking, answer-making, problem-solving animals … above all when we are little."
John Holt

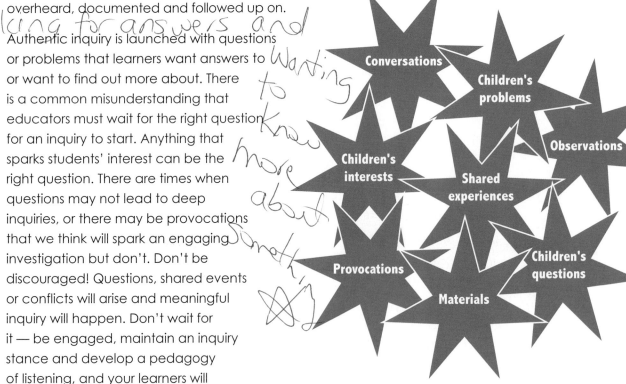

FIGURE 2.1 The inquiry spark can come from many different sources.

Conversations
Children's problems
Observations
Children's interests
Shared experiences
Children's questions
Provocations
Materials

2.2 What is my role in an inquiry-based classroom?

When we look into inquiry-based classrooms, educators are employing many different strategies that allow for authentic questioning and learning to occur.

Talk less and listen more

According to Alfie Kohn, in outstanding classrooms, teachers do more listening than talking and students (children) do more talking than listening. Terrific teachers often have teeth marks on their tongues. Simply put, let the learners do the talking and if you are going to respond, try and make your response a question.

Be open to children's questions

Encourage, welcome and invite children's questions and use the questions to drive inquiry. Let your children know that you are interested and want to hear their questions. This gives voice to learners' ideas.

Ask open questions

Think about the questions you ask — do they allow an entry point for all learners? Ask questions that open up thinking, not close it down. Allow for wait time when learners ask questions and revisit their questions often. When in doubt, say, "Tell me about..."

Notice and name

Make learning and thinking visible by noticing and naming. It allows learners to know why they are doing what they are doing. It also sets the stage for them to be able to notice and name their learning.

Know and honour children's interests

When we know our learners, we can assist them in making connections to prior knowledge and experiences, and support them with their personal inquiries.

Establish a culture that supports wondering

An environment that encourages questions and pondering by both learners and educators means that all thoughts and wonderings are acknowledged and honoured.

Big Idea

Educators must be co-learners who model their wonder and thinking with children.

Capacity

Which of these strategies do you use now and which ones would you like to try or do more often?

Food for Thought

"Developing in students a love of discovery ... should be our aim. To do so, however, teachers and students must have the intellectual freedom to follow the lead of their own questions."

Grant Wiggins

Think aloud

Let your learners hear you thinking out loud about what you are doing and thinking, especially about your wonderings and misconceptions. Think aloud about how you are going to find out about your wondering as well. Modelling is powerful way to engage children in doing it themselves. Educator's wonderings can spark inquiries as well.

Use the power of "co"

Co-create, collaborate, and co-negotiate. Knowing that your children are proficient, talented and intelligent allows you to be a co-learner alongside them, and lets them realize that there are times when they will be leading the learning.

Be responsive, adaptive and flexible

Be open to "going with the flow" of an inquiry. Understand that some inquiries will take off while others with not — and that is okay. Enjoy the surprise and unpredictability of authentic learning.

Use authentic, thought-provoking materials

Offer texts, artifacts, natural and found objects, people, learning experiences and places that instill a sense of wonder and cultivate more questions. Allow children to provide these materials as well, and let them be the "knowledgeable other" when they have expertise.

Take a broad view

Have a deep, working knowledge of conceptual understandings, program expectations, skills, knowledge and child development. This enables educators to support inquiry broadly, scaffold learning, use intentional materials and resources, and ask provoking questions that promote thinking and learning in all areas.

Capacity
What do you think you need to do to embrace the effective practices of inquiry-based educators? Do you require additional information?

FIGURE 2.2 Children's wonder is at the centre of inquiry, but there are many practices educators can use to activate and nurture their learning.

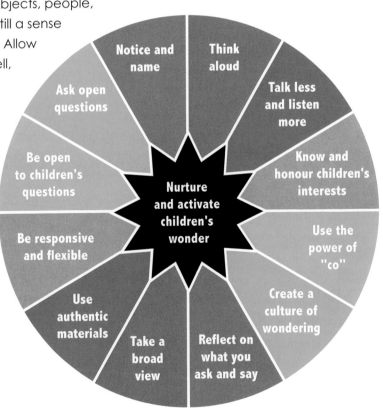

2.3 What are the best kinds of questions for inquiry?

How an educator responds to a child's questions is a skill in itself. It takes a curious and creative mind and heart to start with a student wondering — not quite knowing where it might lead — and transform it into a learning experience.

We play an important part in moving the wonderings forward, engaging those who are interested as well as documenting and assessing learning throughout an inquiry. The challenge at this point on the journey is that there is really not a set plan or course. The wonderings, responses and newly created questions determine the path. As educators, our knowledge of our learners — where they are and where they might go — assists us in being responsive to the inquiry.

As we work through the elements of inquiry, we are discovering and reflecting on the most effective way we can support learners. This may be through additional questioning, providing materials, checking in frequently with children (individually and in small and large groups) as well as teaching when needed. We use our observations and documentation to assist with this.

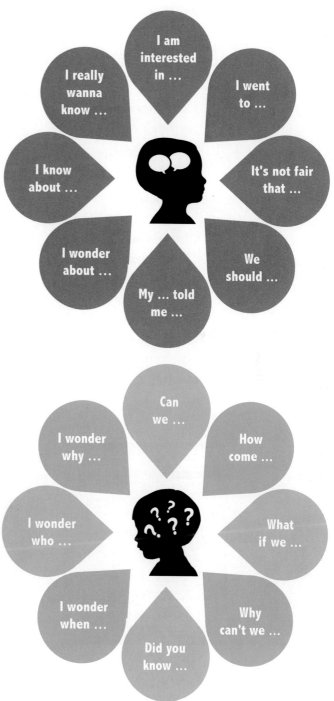

FIGURE 2.3 Listening to and respecting what children ask and say is the most important thing educators can do to create powerful and relevant inquiry experiences for their learners.

What kinds of question prompts should educators use?

Educators can respond to learner's wonderings by building on the initial question with further questions. Reflecting on the questions we ask in response is time well spent. Much research has been done about questioning and asking effective questions. With regards to inquiry in kindergarten, it is often beneficial to respond with "tell me about" or "tell me more." This open-ended questioning allows the child to share at a level that is appropriate for them. The educator can then respond to the child's response.

It is an interesting challenge to record yourself engaging with learners and listening to the questions you are posing. This is an excellent way to note whether your questions have one answer or many, if they have entry points for all, and if they grow curiosity and wondering. Include educator questioning in documentation, as the educator has done in Figure 2.5. Revisiting our recorded conversations is a purposeful way to reflect on and rethink our questioning skills.

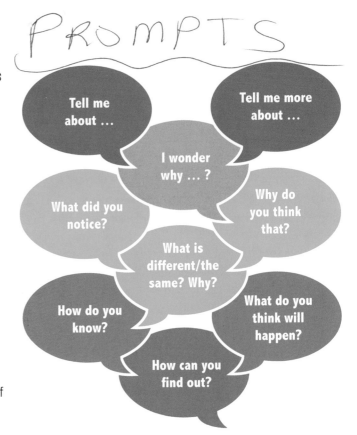

FIGURE 2.4 Educators can respond to learner's wonderings by building on the initial prompt with further questions.

FIGURE 2.5 Posting question prompts in the classroom environment is another way for educators to be aware of the prompts they are using.

FIGURE 2.6 The most effective inquiry questions share common qualities that make them exciting, provocative and intellectually challenging.

2.4 Does every interest, wondering and question become an inquiry?

Big Idea
When launching an inquiry, ask yourself "What?" "So what?" and "Now what?"

This question is often asked by educators trying to create an inquiry-based environment. In fact, it is a common misconception about inquiry: that we choose from the constantly changing and fleeting interests of children. It would be wonderful if we could follow each child's wondering, but we know this is not realistic. So how do we decide? We like the way Ciccone (2016) has used the reflection model of "What? So What? Now What?" to consider if an interest or theory could become an inquiry.

This reflection model can also address the question of how long an inquiry should last. Since inquiry is an in-and-out process, more questions and wonderings constantly arise. We can use the reflection model to help determine if the interest for a topic is still there. Most educators we have worked with say they know when something has come to a close, but also keep in mind that when documentation is revisited, the spark may ignite again. If the inquiry was initiated by a problem, the solving of the problem could mark the close of an inquiry, unless another problem arises.

Educators know their children and can tell when they are engaged and interested; this professional judgment should be applied. But ask your learners! In a community meeting, knowledge circle, or during a discussion about an ongoing inquiry, ask if all questions about the topic have been answered or whether more needs to be uncovered. Remember that some inquires may last just a day or two. Sometimes it may involve the whole class, a small group or an individual child. Therefore, when something is "done," it will look different in each classroom, within groupings or with individuals.

What?

- What is the learner's theory or wondering?
- Is it fleeting or momentary?
- Based on your knowledge of the learner, is it something they seem truly curious about?

So what?

- Is this an important question?
- What is the most substantial aspect?
- Can it be linked to prior knowledge?
- Are there connections to curriculum?
- Can new knowledge be built?
- Could learners make their thinking visible?
- Can it be connected to something in real life?

Now what?

- What do those interested already know or think about the wondering?
- Where do we hope to go?
- How will we co-plan and co-negotiate?
- What materials/resources are needed?
- Who will provide them?
- How will we capture children's thinking and learning?
- How will we revisit this thinking and learning?

FIGURE 2.7 This reflection model can help decide when to initiate, pursue or conclude an inquiry.

The marble dilemma

What?

A group of learners in Meghan's class loved the marble run. It was a popular item in the classroom and was used extensively each day. After a marble swallowing incident that turned out to be a false alarm, the marbles were put away for a while. Many of the children were disappointed and asked repeatedly for the marble run.

So what?

Meghan gathered the children and said they could have a ping pong ball if they wanted to build their own run. She made a connection to a real-life situation and shared a provocation with her learners. Immediately a number of students began planning — they were committed to solving their problem. Meghan could see that there were many possible connections to conceptual understandings and big ideas. She was confident that new knowledge would be built as the learners began creating their new run. She began thinking about the opportunities that would arise for learners to make their thinking visible and how she would document that learning.

Now what?

Initially the children asked for paper towel rolls and ping pong balls, but soon found the balls were "too big to move through the rolls." Those involved in the inquiry had a meeting with Meghan and told her what they needed: "Construction paper and lots of duct tape!" They created tubes with black construction paper, working together

to ensure that the ping pong ball "fitted." They had to solve the problem of how they were going to get the ball to "run down" liked it did in the other run. One of the learners suggested that it had to be up high, but how were they going to keep it up high? "Someone just can't keep standing here and holding it." One of the learners had the idea to have it "run from the chalk ledge." They tried this and found that it worked better if it ran "on an angle from the bulletin board." After they constructed the first straight tube, they added other tubes to make the run more complex. It took a number of days of problem-solving and collaboration, but soon their Ball Track was ready to use. Problem solved!

2.5 What types of provocations can I use?

There are many different methods, strategies, tools and techniques educators can employ to provoke an inquiry with their young learners. In this chapter we examine some of the approaches and experiences that have worked for educators we have spoken with. The best ones are those that, on any given day, evoke the most powerful responses from your learners. If one approach isn't working, you have many more you can employ.

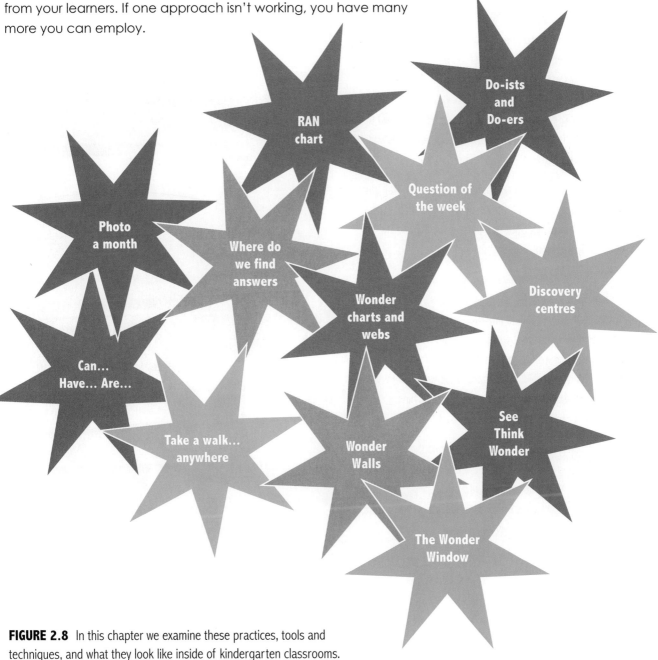

FIGURE 2.8 In this chapter we examine these practices, tools and techniques, and what they look like inside of kindergarten classrooms.

Wonder Walls

Wonder Walls are a space where learners can post their questions and wonderings. Educators we work with have said Wonder Walls are most effective when learners help determine where the space is and the practise of using them is modeled consistently. It is also important to revisit the Wonder Wall frequently. This space needs to be fluid and dynamic, so that both learners and educators use it purposefully to inform inquiry pathways. Sticky notes or paper and writing tools could also be provided so that learners, educators or classroom visitors can record their answers to the wonderings or perhaps pose other questions. The wonderings could also be used to set up intentional discovery centres with materials and resources reflective of the questions on the wall.

These wonderings in were posted on a Wonder Wall after the educators had read a book about the ocean. This sparked an inquiry about underwater creatures. The children's questions initiated the inquiry and it grew from there.

Notice that all learners can post on the wall regardless of where they are developmentally with their writing. Kegan's question about trees was posted at the same time. Her wondering could be filed with her documentation and revisited later, educators could ask if any other children are interested, or possibly Kegan could do some investigating on her own.

When creating a culture of inquiry, part of the understanding is that not all questions can be explored immediately. Negotiation may need to happen; consensus may need to be reached with the understanding that the wondering will not be forgotten.

This would be a great teacher/student initiated one for September

Wonder charts and webs

These are recordings of children's wonderings and are similar to Wonder Walls. It is interesting to do them a number of times during an inquiry as answers and more questions are created. Keeping the charts and webs posted allows everyone to see the pathway of the inquiry, where it might go next, and makes thinking and learning visible.

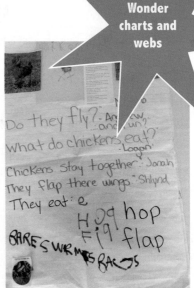

Wonder charts and webs

Leaf Inquiry = Change

Take a walk... anywhere

Getting out of the classroom and going outdoors, somewhere else in the school or on a trip is an excellent way to provoke wonderings. Traditionally, these types of experiences were often done at the end of a theme or unit of study. If we flip our thinking around and use these experiences to launch an inquiry, the avenues are endless.

Take a walk... anywhere

These wonderings were sparked during a walk outside to collect leaves. Each learner collected a number of leaves and shared their wonderings. A community circle was formed to discuss the questions posed. Some of the leaners had answers to their co-learner's questions. Materials were provided by both the educators and the learners to investigate the life of leaves. Stewardship was a focus, as well as the idea that life is a cycle and that humans are often a part of the cycle for other living things.

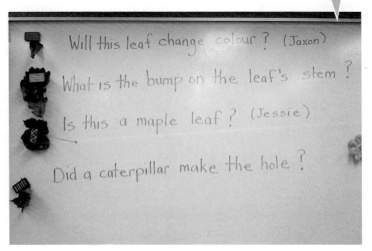

See
Think
Wonder

See Think Wonder... about the Olympics

Another powerful framework for inquiry is See Think Wonder. Included with these prompts is the prompt, "What makes you think that?" This framework can be used with a picture, photo, artifact, video clip or a natural object. The following narrative is how an educator team used See Think Wonder to spark an in-depth inquiry on the Winter Olympics.

Sue and Anne used the See Think Wonder framework to support student interest in the Winter Olympics in Sochi. Both educators had done Olympic themes in the past and wanted to move beyond the traditional exploration of countries and flags.

Ski hill:
What do you see?
What do you think?
What do you wonder?

Day 1: Sue and Anne started with a projected photo of the ski hill and posed the questions, "What do you see," "What do you wonder," "What are you thinking" and "What makes you say that?" The children responded with all kinds of thoughts about what it was, how it was built and how fast it would be. Eventually the conversation turned to the question, "Where do the athletes stay when they go to the Olympics?"

Day 2: The next day the team projected the photo of the Athlete's Village and asked the same questions. Again, the discussion was rich with thoughts and opinions. "What were the rooms like?" "Where did they eat?" "Did all the countries stay together in the same house?" "Did they miss their moms?" A group of students started to talk about building their own Olympic Village. They discussed what they would need and began to plan how they would build it. Other groups of students decided they would create the athletes and equipment for the village and others decided they wanted to make the Olympic rings to decorate the village. Soon one whole area of the classroom was dedicated to the Olympics inquiry.

Athletes' village:
What do you see?
What do you think?
What do you wonder?

Children were bringing in materials from home to add to the inquiry area, as well as articles from the newspaper with factual information which they posted and wrote about. They explored race times, speeds and medal counts. Sue and Anne had frequent check-ins with the children about what they were creating and thinking about.

Beginning construction of the village

See Think Wonder, cont'd

This was also an opportunity to discuss the knowledge that was being created and where the inquiry might go next. In the end the class decided to team up with another K class and hold their own Winter Olympics.

Based on much of the learning they did during their inquiry, they devised plans for their own event. They created an Olympic torch and each child ran with the torch. They brainstormed what events they would have and who the judges would be. They constructed medal podiums and designed medals. They displayed dispositions of perseverance, teamwork, creativity, passion and commitment, much like Olympic athletes. The educators made broader connections between the student's hard work and learning and what dedicated athletes had to do to make it to the Olympics. A month of thinking and learning was born out of a general interest about a global event and the prompts to see, think and wonder.

More construction

The village

Ski racer ready at the start gate

Bobsledders

An Olympic event

Cookie sheet ice rink and skates made from paper clips

Question of the week/day/month

The question of the week centre could be placed anywhere in the environment. Questions of the week could be taken from the Wonder Wall or be a question posed by educators. Learners love it when their wondering is the question of the week. Time is given each week to share responses to the question and to do some research to discover answers. This experience allows for educators to model where answers to questions can be found.

We have found that when children see the question at the start of the week, they engage their families as well. Experts on topics can be found everywhere.

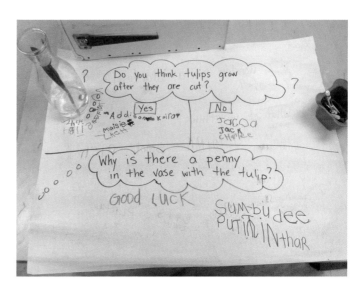

This was a question of the week that educator Cara posed to her class because it was a wondering that she had after seeing cut tulips in a vase. Upon reflection, she realized that her initial question could only be answered with "yes" or "no," so she added a second question that was much more open. In fact, tulips can grow up to an inch after being cut!

Photo a month

This is a good provocation for an inquiry that can start in September and go until June. Choose a spot outside of the school and take a photo of the class in that spot every month of the school year. These photos are a great way to initiate a discussion and ongoing inquiry about seasonal changes and stewardship.

This educator took a photo of the class under the same tree in the schoolyard each month. It was a great ongoing inquiry that all the learners took part in.

Discovery centres with intentional materials

This is another simple yet effective way to get learners discussing and wondering. Tables or spaces can be set up with intentional materials such as texts, artifacts, objects from nature, loose parts, a class plant or pet, or photos. A video could even be played on a loop. Questions could be posed or not posed. Observation journals can be left out for learners to discuss wonderings. Discovery centres are a good place for educators to observe and document conversations that are happening and ask open-ended questions. Educators could then invite further thinking by sharing what they heard with the group: "Today at the discovery table I heard Emmett talking about… What do you know about…? How could we find out about what Emmett is wondering?"

Discovery centres

Box of mixed materials: "Make a balanced structure."

Tray of snow: "How long will it take to melt?"

Class plant, clipboard and pens: "How much has it grown?"

Corn cobs and paint

Gourds and spoons

Loose parts

Live discoveries

Inquiry Jump off Lesson

The Wonder or Observation Window

This idea comes from *A Place for Wonder* by Heard and McDonough. It is simple and inexpensive, and provides an ever-changing view for wonderings that can be used as provocations for inquiry.

A Wonder Window is created by taping off a square or any shape on a classroom window and leaving a journal there so that learners can share their thoughts and wonderings. Educators can use these wonderings as provocations for inquiries. If you are lucky enough to have windows that face different directions in your room, then two Wonder Windows allow for comparison. Placing a bird feeder or a plant in the window adds to the experience.

The Wonder Window in Meghan's class had a frequent visitor, which sparked an interest in black-capped chickadees and other winter birds, and what birds do when the weather changes.

Where do we find answers?

This is a lesson that can be taught explicitly and revisited later. With wondering comes the question, "How do we find answers?" This is an excellent question to pose to learners. An anchor chart that lists sources for answers can be co-created. The chart is then posted in the classroom and can be added to when new resources are discovered. It can be referred to frequently during inquiry experiences by both educators and learners.

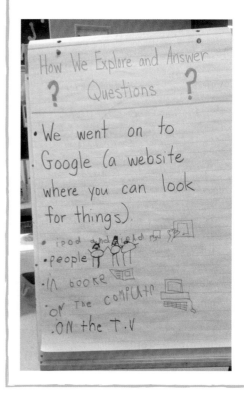

The wonderings of Do-ists and Do-ers

This idea was created by two educators who wanted to support their learners in asking a greater variety of questions. This seemed very challenging for their class. Together they talked about what kinds of people ask questions and decided to expand on this idea. They listed "ists": scientists, archaeologists, chemists, biologists, artists, gymnasts, etc. They also listed "ers": dancers, doctors, swimmers, writers, hairdressers, etc. They gathered texts and resources about these roles, read them, and displayed them in the classroom. The educators created a slideshow and asked the learners what kinds of questions these people might ask. It got the juices flowing and when children asked questions, the educators would say, "That is the kind of question an engineer might ask." This modelled language became the language the children would use as well.

Some scientists study animals. This scientist is a zoologist.

Some scientists study the human body and help us stay healthy. This scientist is a doctor.

Do-ists and Do-ers

RAN chart (Reading and Analysing Non-fiction)

This template comes from Tony Stead's book *Reality Checks* (2005) and is an excellent alternative to the KWL. The RAN chart explores prior knowledge, but it also addresses misconceptions that learners may have. These misconceptions are often a great way to dig deep into an inquiry so that thinking can be challenged and new knowledge can be built. The KWL chart includes the following categories:

RAN chart

What we know	What we want to know	What we learned

The RAN chart adds two more elements to the framework: Educators or learners can write the facts that they think they know about a topic on sticky notes and these notes can be moved to other columns as the inquiry grows.

What we think we know	Yes! We were right	Misconceptions	New information	Still wondering

Can... Have... Are...

When a wondering is shared or an idea for study is proposed, a great way to explore prior knowledge is the framework of Can... Have... Are.... This allows both learners and educators to examine what they already know about something and where they might go next in the inquiry. It is also a way that misconceptions can be addressed.

Frances and Vanessa used the Can... Have... Are... framework to lay the foundation for an inquiry about caterpillars and butterflies. All thoughts and ideas are honoured as prior knowledge is shared and recorded. In this example the educators did the recording.

Butterflies...

Can... go to Mexico, land on flowers, come out of a chrysalis

Have... heads, wings, polka dots

Are... caterpillars, pretty, beautiful

Caterpillars...

Can... eat leaves, turn into butterflies, wriggle

Have... lots of legs, eggs, fur

Are... soft, cuddly, round like a ball, butterflies

Can...
Have... Are...

THINQ

- Which of these provocation strategies are new to you and might you like to try?

- Which of these provocation strategies have you tried and how successful have they been in provoking student wonderings?

Context

What are your learners most curious about? What kinds of provocations might activate their thinking?

2.6 What if my learners aren't interested in the inquiry we are doing?

Big Idea
Take a deep breath and let the learner's curiosity lead.

We know the following about our learners: that they have innate curiosity and are proficient, talented and intelligent; that when we have learning environments with engaging materials that are intentionally placed, learner curiosity can be supported and grown; and that when they are engaged in play, inquiry is happening, and when they are engaged in inquiry, they are playing.

Conviction
If, during inquiry, your expectations for children's learning are not met, does this undermine your belief in the power of inquiry-based learning? What keeps you going?

If the whole class is not participating in an inquiry, what are the other children doing? Most likely they are engaged at discovery centres, or with materials that have been thoughtfully chosen to develop and grow skills that are similar and quite possibly the same as the skills that are developed with inquiry. Not every child is going to have a burning interest to be engaged in every inquiry that is happening, and that's okay.

Mini-inquiries are happening each day at the blocks, the art studio, or the sand table — everywhere in a kindergarten classroom. Educators are observing and documenting this thinking, and learning and asking open-ended questions that lead towards next steps, just as we do with inquiry.

We also need to consider the development stages of our learners when we reflect on why they might not be interested in an inquiry. Do they prefer solitary or parallel play to cooperative play? What is their oral language like? If they prefer playing in one area with one material, do you know why? Could these preferences be a part of an inquiry? The most effective approach is knowing our students, their interests, dispositions and learning styles; listening and observing; offering engaging provocations; and taking a deep breath and letting our learner's curiosity lead us.

[handwritten note: Developmental Stages some JKs might not be ready]

THINQ

- How can you step back, observe, and notice and name, when inquiries are happening in your classroom on a daily basis?

- What is your greatest challenge with respect to the flow of inquiry in your classroom? Have you considered the interests and developmental stages of the children?

Revisit and reflect

In this chapter we looked at wondering and questioning in an inquiry classroom, and how educators can model their own wondering and thinking. We explored the fact that the best questions come from our learners and discussed ways to support this. We offered a variety of strategies, tools and techniques to provoke inquiry, and provided in-class examples of each of them. Finally, we propose that educators take a deep breath and let children's curiosity lead the way.

THINQ

- What new provocation strategies and ideas from this chapter are you going to try in your classroom?

- With whom would you want to share Reproducible 2A, *6 big ideas about wondering and questioning in kindergarten*?

- Could you and your colleagues use Reproducible 2B, *12 practices, tools and techniques to provoke inquiry in kindergarten classrooms* as the basis for a collaborative inquiry project?

- Where could you place Reproducible 2C, *8 characteristics of robust inquiry questions* as a reminder of what makes a good question?

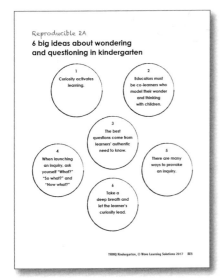

FIGURE 2.9 Reproducible 2A, p. RE5.

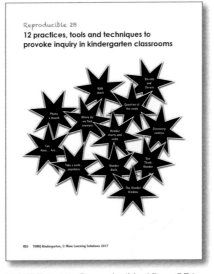

FIGURE 2.10 Reproducible 2B, p. RE6.

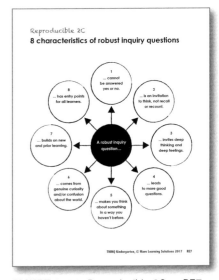

FIGURE 2.11 Reproducible 2C, p. RE7.

Chapter 3

CREATING AN INQUIRY ENVIRONMENT:
The context for learning

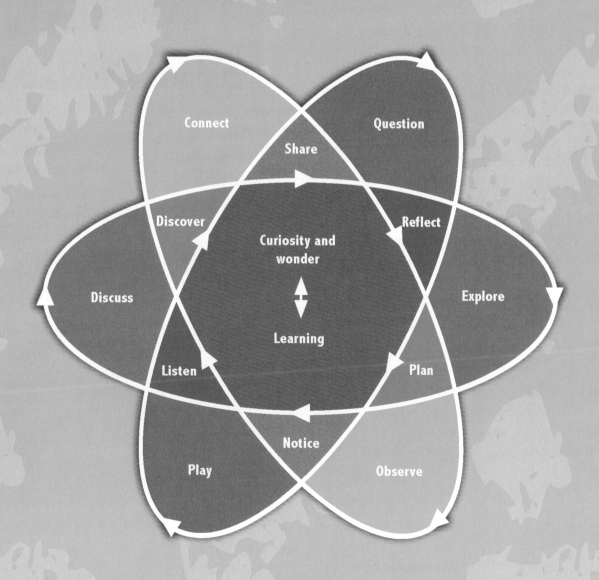

3.1 What is an inquiry-based environment?

When we say the environment is the "context" in which learning takes place, we are talking about the conditions for learning, such as time, space and materials. Context also includes consideration of community, culture and atmosphere in the classroom. The "environment" in kindergarten is often referred to as the "third teacher." If we consider the environment as a third teacher, what role does it play in an inquiry-based classroom? Educators and researchers like Lella Gandini, Susan Fraser and Margie Carter have proposed that the environment reinforces thinking and learning, "respon[ding] to student interests and provid[ing] opportunities for students to make their thinking visible." This means that both the physical space and the culture established within the space are important.

We want to provide learning environments that provoke curiosity and wonder, generate intellectual challenges, and create a sense of belonging. As we think about and co-create our learning environments, we must support learning for both children and educators. It is important to consistently reflect on how our intentions and knowledge of our learners is affecting the learning environments we create. This means that "we are not decorating learning spaces, we are designing them to amplify learning" (Hare and Dillon).

So, the spaces we create are reflections of who we are and what we believe and value. We can begin to reflect on a kindergarten inquiry-based environment by examining our own beliefs about young children, their relationships, learning and inquiry.

Inquiry in Action

The environment, beliefs and values

What beliefs and values about inquiry, learning and children do you see reflected in these classrooms?

A reflective space

Materials are accessible

Furniture can be used for many purposes

If beliefs and values are the foundation of created spaces, how do the statements in Figure 3.1 reflect your thinking about an inquiry-based environment? You can discuss these values with your colleagues by sharing Reproducible 3A, *Considering educator values and the learning environment.*

> **Capacity**
> How convinced are you that your values influence the learning environment?

Reflecting on values and the environment

Do you share the following values?

- Young children are proficient, talented and intelligent.
- Young children are capable of identifying themselves as concerned, kind, considerate, caring, thoughtful and imaginative citizens.
- Educators model and support a stance of inquiry and wonder.
- A learning environment is co-planned and co-created.
- Educators are intentional with words, actions and experiences so that children know why and what they are doing, and how to do it.
- All voices are honoured, and self-efficacy and ownership is built.
- Questioning is encouraged and supported.
- Ongoing collaboration and communication is encouraged.
- Inquiry flows throughout the day and is not subject-specific.
- Explicit teaching of skills and knowledge is done in the context of an inquiry environment.
- An inquiry-based environment supports learning that is authentic, purpose-driven and engaging.
- The structuring of time and space supports deep thinking and learning.
- Materials are chosen purposefully to support thinking and learning.
- Learners understand the intentionality of the materials.
- A co-learning relationship amongst educators, children and families supports inquiry.
- A negotiated curriculum in inquiry begins with the interests of children.

FIGURE 3.1 If beliefs and values are the foundation of created learning spaces and environments, how well do these statements reflect your thinking about an inquiry-based environment?

> **Food for Thought**
> "Respect for the image of the child as rich, strong, and powerful is fundamental in preparing an environment that allows the child to be actively engaged in the process of learning."
> Susan Fraser

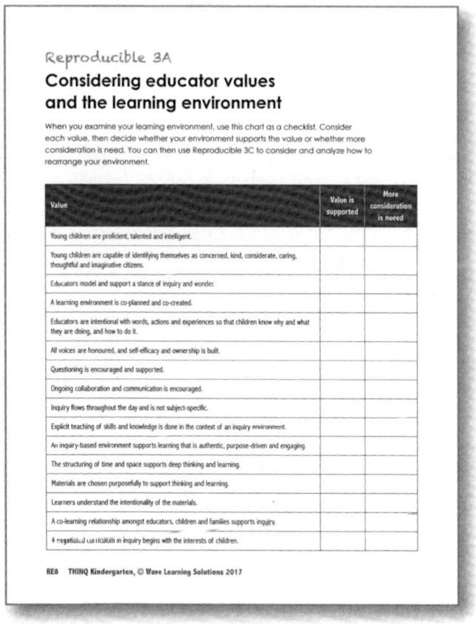

Reproducible 3A

Considering educator values and the learning environment

When you examine your learning environment, use this chart as a checklist. Consider each value, then decide whether your environment supports the value or whether more consideration is need. You can then use Reproducible 3C to consider and analyze how to rearrange your environment.

Value	Value is supported	More consideration is neeed
Young children are proficient, talented and intelligent.		
Young children are capable of identifying themselves as concerned, kind, considerate, caring, thoughtful and imaginative citizens.		
Educators model and support a stance of inquiry and wonder.		
A learning environment is co-planned and co-created.		
Educators are intentional with words, actions and experiences so that children know why and what they are doing, and how to do it.		
All voices are honoured, and self-efficacy and ownership is built.		
Questioning is encouraged and supported.		
Ongoing collaboration and communication is encouraged.		
Inquiry flows throughout the day and is not subject-specific.		
Explicit teaching of skills and knowledge is done in the context of an inquiry environment.		
An inquiry-based environment supports learning that is authentic, purpose-driven and engaging.		
The structuring of time and space supports deep thinking and learning.		
Materials are chosen purposefully to support thinking and learning.		
Learners understand the intentionality of the materials.		
A co-learning relationship amongst educators, children and families supports inquiry.		
A negotiated curriculum in inquiry begins with the interests of children.		

RE8 THINQ Kindergarten, © Wave Learning Solutions 2017

FIGURE 3.2 Reproducible 3A, p. RE8.

3.2 What kind of culture best supports an effective inquiry-based classroom?

Big Idea

An inquiry environment includes the culture or tone of the classroom.

As we discussed in previous chapters, the stance an educator takes towards inquiry has great bearing on how inquiry is embraced in a classroom. When we model and think aloud about our own wonderings, misconceptions and search for knowledge, our children realize these actions are what inquiring learners do. Creating a safe and inclusive environment for questioning and exploring begins with educators who question and explore themselves. Noticing and naming inquiry dispositions validates and celebrates these actions.

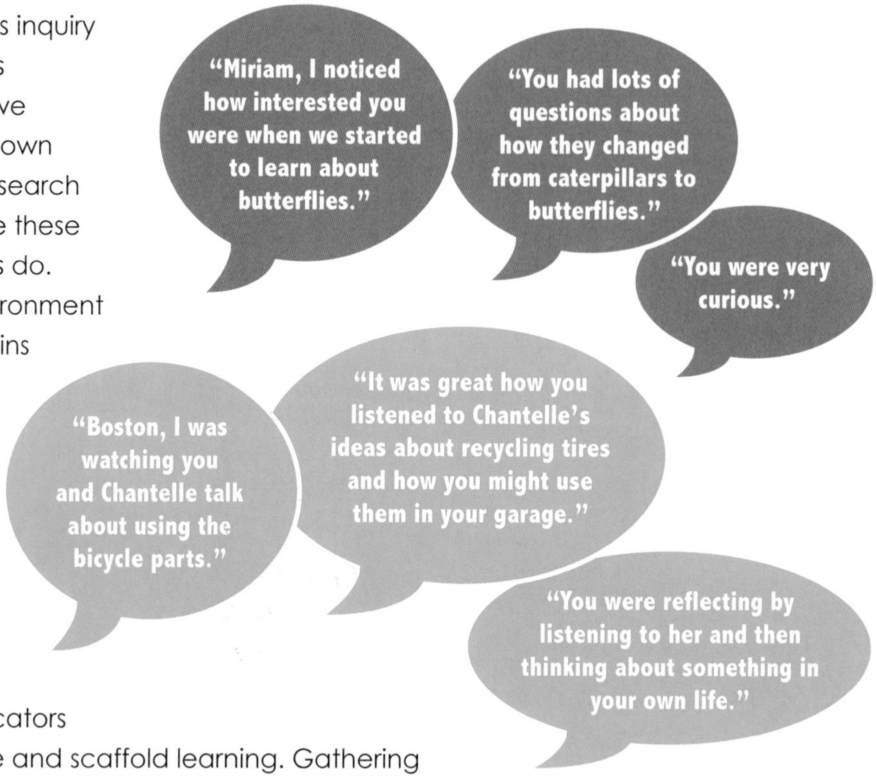
"Miriam, I noticed how interested you were when we started to learn about butterflies."
"You had lots of questions about how they changed from caterpillars to butterflies."
"You were very curious."
"Boston, I was watching you and Chantelle talk about using the bicycle parts."
"It was great how you listened to Chantelle's ideas about recycling tires and how you might use them in your garage."
"You were reflecting by listening to her and then thinking about something in your own life."

FIGURE 3.3 What is said and how it is said are critical parts of any inquiry-based classroom environment.

Establishing norms

When establishing a culture of inquiry, there are times when educators will need to explicitly model, guide and scaffold learning. Gathering learners for community meetings and discussions to reflect on "how things are going" is vital in establishing a community that thinks and learns together. Educators have shared that there are a number of tensions and challenges that may arise with inquiry. These can include collaborating effectively, sharing ideas and materials, and responding to questions. We have found that learners often need to explicitly explore, discuss and reflect on what these behaviours look like in an inquiry-based environment. Gathering to co-create and record a shared understanding of what collaboration, sharing or questioning looks, sounds and feels like in a classroom can help to anchor children's comprehension of these concepts. Using the children's own pictures and words gives them ownership and values their voice. Co-creating anchor charts as needs or issues arise is a way that educators can be responsive to what is happening in the environment. Posting the anchor chart in a place where it can be referred to by both children and educators helps the norms to become internalized.

Conviction

How convinced are you that reflection and sharing can deepen learning?

Time to share and reflect

A time for educators and learners to gather, discuss and reflect on the experiences and learning that have taken place is important in an inquiry-based classroom for a number of reasons. It helps build the understanding that all are part of the learning community and that everyone's voice and presence is important as an inquiry is negotiated and knowledge is co-constructed. It also allows educators and children the opportunity to focus on what has been discovered, how discoveries were made and what the next steps might be. *Natural Curiosity* (2011) calls these gatherings "knowledge-building circles." Educators also refer to them as community gatherings or sharing circles.

There are many ways in which children can share their thinking at these times, including oral discussion, sharing artifacts, and discussing photos or video. As interactions take place, educators can respond to learner's ideas, shed light on their theories, make connections, and challenge and extend thinking. Children can do the same. It is also a time when educators can share what they have noticed and named, model questioning, and provide feedback. Choices can be made together about what materials and resources may be needed to further the inquiry.

Meaningful observations and documentation can also be done during reflection time. When educators listen to learners share, they can make connections to conceptual understandings and program expectations. These observations can be included in the documentation and assist in determining what explicit teaching or supports are required for both the group and individual children.

Establishing time for these types of gatherings ensures that we can be responsive to the learning and questions that are happening in the moment. These gatherings should happen frequently throughout an inquiry. We know that knowledge is a social construct and this is a time when shared experiences and knowledge can foster new learning and understanding. Norms may also need to be established and explicitly modelled for these reflection times so that conversations and discussions are meaningful for all.

Inquiry in Action

Time to reflect

Sue and Ann noticed that some of their learners were having difficulty moving forward with inquiry because they found it difficult to share their materials and listen to others talking about their ideas. The educators were spending a lot of time intervening and redirecting behaviour, so they decided to have a community meeting. When the children were gathered, Sue and Ann talked with learners about the things they were noticing. They proposed that they talk about what listening and sharing looked, sounded and felt like. The topic of cooperation and what it was came up as well. There was lots of honest discussion and over the week Sue, Ann and the children co-created a chart that captured what they thought listening, sharing and including looked, sounded and felt like. With modeling, guidance, and regular referrals to the chart, everyone felt like things were going much better. The educators were spending less time intervening and had more time to observe and purposefully engage the learners, and the learners were self-regulating independently.

Co-created cooperation chart

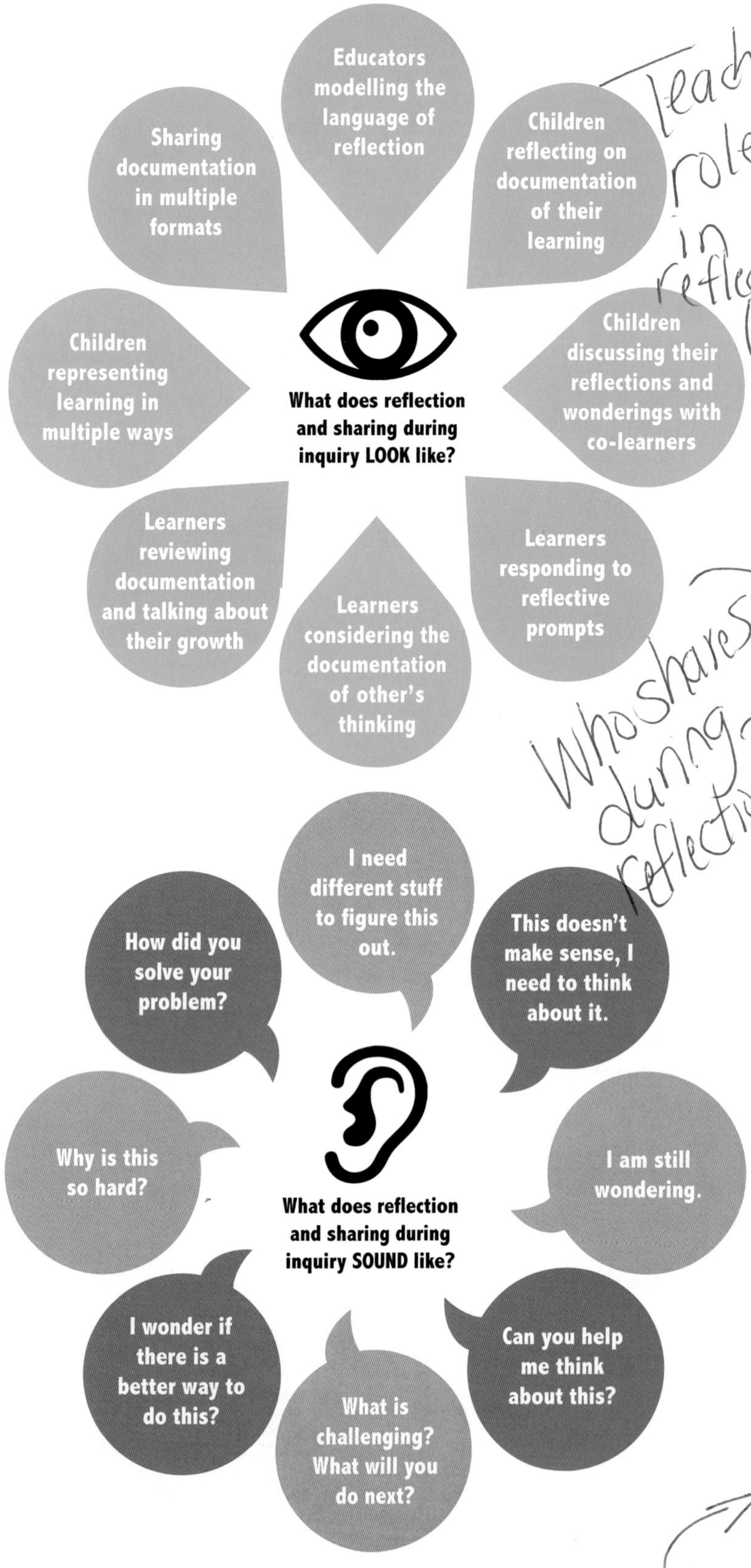

What does reflection and sharing during inquiry LOOK like?

- Educators modelling the language of reflection
- Children reflecting on documentation of their learning
- Children discussing their reflections and wonderings with co-learners
- Learners responding to reflective prompts
- Learners considering the documentation of other's thinking
- Learners reviewing documentation and talking about their growth
- Children representing learning in multiple ways
- Sharing documentation in multiple formats

What does reflection and sharing during inquiry SOUND like?

- How did you solve your problem?
- I need different stuff to figure this out.
- This doesn't make sense, I need to think about it.
- I am still wondering.
- Can you help me think about this?
- What is challenging? What will you do next?
- I wonder if there is a better way to do this?
- Why is this so hard?

Handwritten note: Teacher role in reflection

Handwritten note: Who shares during reflection?

FIGURE 3.4 The sights and sounds of inquiry reflection and sharing are concrete.

Alexis discusses reflection and sharing time

"Reflection time is a crucial part of our day. Reflection time is when we gather as a group to share our learning from discovery time. I jokingly refer to reflection time as 'free advertising' because it is the time when we can highlight the important learning goals, behaviours and discoveries we want the children to be demonstrating through the children's own work."

"The decision about which children share is not random, but purposeful. Perhaps it might be a student who made a breakthrough or did their personal best, or it may be a child sharing an interesting way they interacted with materials at one of our provocations, or it may be a child sharing a problem they encountered while working and the class is invited to help them brainstorm a solution."

"The reflection process is interactive. When a child is sharing, the class is given the opportunity to ask questions and give feedback. I continue to be amazed by how thoughtful the children are in their questions and comments. They often speak of being 'inspired' by things they saw their classmates doing. I am often inspired too! And what about the child who chooses the same centre day after day? Reflection time is one of the ways we can inspire that child to try something new, or at the very least, stay connected to all the interesting things that are happening in the class."

Handwritten note: For child who chooses same play everyday

3.3 How can I use the physical environment to support inquiry?

Big Idea
The use of time, space and materials needs to be purposeful.

The physical environment in our classrooms is responsive when it is co-constructed to build and sustain meaningful exploration and active engagement. Educators should utilize their knowledge of their student's dispositions, wonderings and abilities when planning and creating the learning environment. When we think about environments where children feel welcomed, safe and encouraged to inquire, there are a number of characteristics that they share.

Space and materials

When decisions about materials, set-up and experiences are shared, learners take ownership of their environment and can see themselves reflected in it.

Rethinking and repurposing materials

Spaces should be flexible and adaptable to meet the needs of the co-learners in the class. Tables, shelves and larger pieces of equipment should be selected because they can serve multiple purposes. A table could be used for loose parts or become part of an airplane that is being constructed for an inquiry. A table made for water or sand could hold any kind of material depending on the inquiry or the interests of the children at the time.

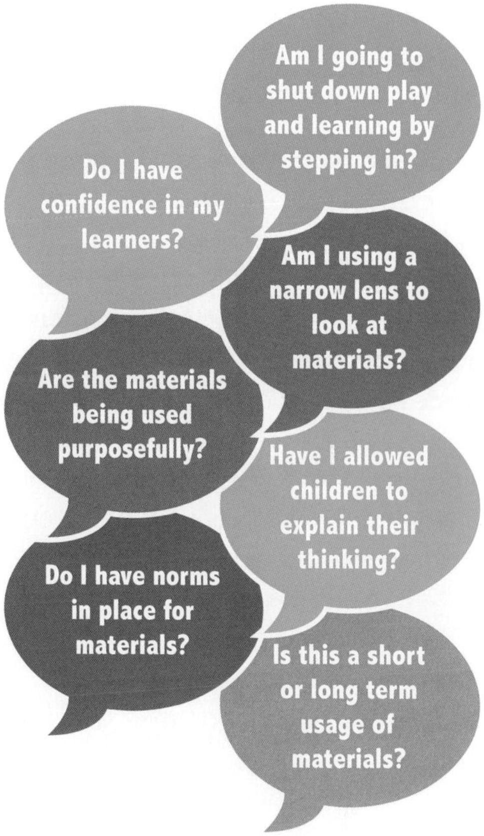

Am I going to shut down play and learning by stepping in?
Do I have confidence in my learners?
Am I using a narrow lens to look at materials?
Are the materials being used purposefully?
Have I allowed children to explain their thinking?
Do I have norms in place for materials?
Is this a short or long term usage of materials?

FIGURE 3.5 Before you step in and request that children comply with an educator-imposed rule about materials, will you stop and reflect on these questions?

FIGURE 3.6 Learners drew up a plan of a plane's cockpit and spoke to the school custodian about what they could use from the storage room. They created a radar from a clock, a gearshift from some piping and a gas pedal from a garbage can. A table and chairs become the control panel and the seats for the pilot and co-pilot.

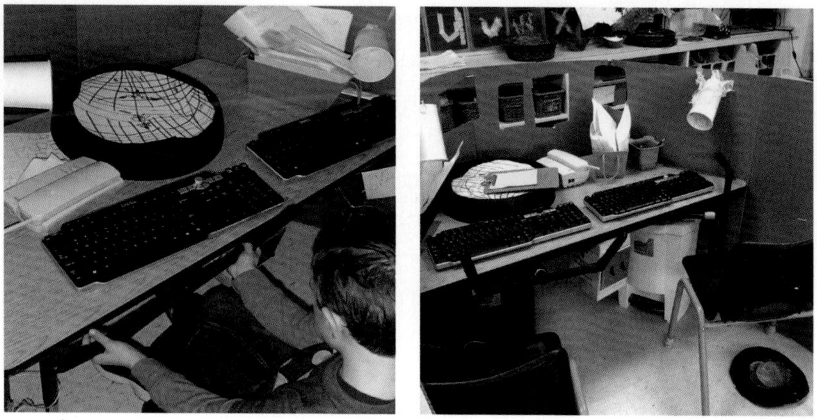

Spaces for gathering

Effective environments should have space for both large and small group gatherings to discuss learning. Examine your space and reflect on whether there are places for the many ways learning can happen with inquiry. Is there a place for playing, exploring, discovering, planning, observing, sharing, listening, questioning, reflecting and making connections? Do the materials in these spaces support this learning?

Removing materials to make space

Think about removing materials that are not purposeful at the time, or for the specific inquiry. Perhaps there are furniture or materials that have always been in the space but are not used by either educators or learners. Could they be removed or repurposed? When we remove pieces that are not used and then reintroduce them at a later time, our children often find new uses for them. If possible, these pieces might take on another role in the outdoor environment. We also need to consider if children can access the materials independently and have a role in deciding where materials are placed, as well as providing and suggesting materials. Materials that provoke inquiry are meaningful, inclusive and open-ended, and will change over time to reflect the interests and inquiries learners are engaged in.

Materials as provocations

Educators can consider what materials might be placed in the environment as a provocation for or within an inquiry. Educators can simply place materials in the environment or they might model the use of them. Children could also model how they use the materials. When materials can be reimagined and used for multiple purposes, we must be ready for learners to use them in new and different ways. This might mean that wooden blocks become a structure in the water table, play dough becomes muffin dough at a restaurant, or cotton balls are used as marshmallows for a campout. If we think about integrating the areas of learning, we also need to think about integrating materials into different learning experiences. Inquiry can be intellectually messy and may also look messy in a learning space.

FIGURE 3.7 Corn cobs are used as painting tools.

FIGURE 3.8 A water table placed outdoors becomes a hockey rink for a winter sport inquiry.

Posting voices and beliefs

A learning environment should be the voice of the learners that are in it. Documentation and artifacts should be chosen to reflect the learning that has happened, is happening, or is about to happen. This says that what children are doing is the most important part of the space. Children should have a role in deciding what documentation is posted, and their voice and growth should be visible in the documentation. Safety is always a consideration in a kindergarten setting. Feeling safe includes not just physical safety, but also the feeling that it is safe to be a learner, to question and wonder, and to be in charge of one's own learning.

When we post our own educator beliefs in the environment, we are making what is valued known. We have seen this in a variety of ways in kindergarten classes. Poems, question prompts, photos, articles, and sharing of conceptual ideas or program principles in the learning space makes visible to the whole community what is important.

FIGURE 3.9 The materials we offer as inquiry provocations reflect our beliefs about learners. When we believe they are capable, proficient and imaginative citizens, we know that as co-learners they can use a variety of materials in safe and innovative ways.

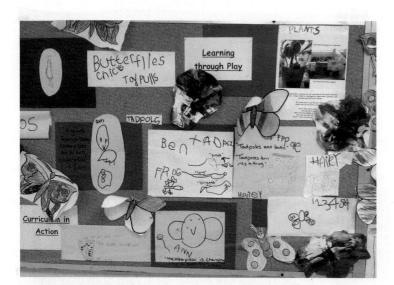

FIGURE 3.10 This board sends a number of messages about the educators' beliefs. Learners' thinking and learning is represented in multiple ways. Student voices are evident in the documentation. The titles "Learning through Play" and "Curriculum in Action" communicates that these are pedagogies the educators honour.

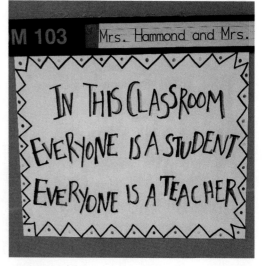

FIGURE 3.11 This message is posted on a classroom door. The belief of the educators is made known upon entering the environment.

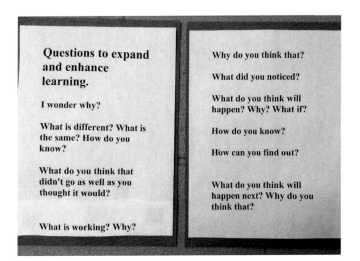

Questions to expand and enhance learning.

I wonder why?

What is different? What is the same? How do you know?

What do you think that didn't go as well as you thought it would?

What is working? Why?

Why do you think that?

What did you noticed?

What do you think will happen? Why? What if?

How do you know?

How can you find out?

What do you think will happen next? Why do you think that?

FIGURE 3.12 Questions to provoke inquiry are posted for both educators and learners.

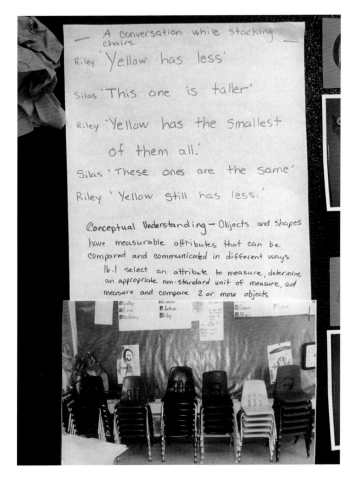

FIGURE 3.13 Posting documentation of a variety of learning experiences communicates that educators understand that learning happens all day long and in multiple ways. This piece of documentation captures Silas and Riley's thinking as they were stacking chairs at the end of the kindergarten day.

Posting for parents

In Alexis's class it is evident that parents are important contributors to a child's learning. A wish ticket and collaborative art piece by learners and their parents are featured in the environment.

Wish tickets for parents

Collaborative art piece

3.4 How can I use the outdoor environment to support inquiry?

Time spent outside is not just for recess, but should be built into the flow of a kindergarten day. We know that children construct knowledge in all environments, so providing inviting and intentional outdoor learning spaces makes good sense. If we rethink the outdoors and learning materials, most of what we do within the four walls of a classroom can be done in an outdoor space.

Year-long outdoor learning provides children a chance to experience natural phenomena such as seasonal changes, rain, snow, sleet, sun, shadows and the changing landscape around them. Time spent learning outdoors provides a rich multi-sensory experience for children. All five sense are stimulated in a way that does not happen indoors.

One of the best things about the outdoor classroom is that it enables learners to move more freely, and for many of our learners this is crucial. Regardless of whether the space is grassy, wooded or paved, children will have daily contact with nature, and a natural and authentic way to provoke inquiry. Bugs, grass, dirt, sticks, stones and puddles all come at no cost, which is another appealing feature of outdoor learning.

Maynard and Waters found that learning outdoors provides positive growth in the areas of problem solving, social skills and cognitive development. An outdoor environment also offers experiences for those with different learning styles. They also noted that children who spend time learning outdoors develop their potential to be aware of and care for the wider environment. Life-long learning about stewardship and how we can care for our world and living things is nurtured when children spend time outdoors. As educators we can introduce, promote and co-learn these important concepts with our learners.

Research in favour of outdoor learning "

Chase learned that rocks make a good paper weight. When the wind started to blow our art around he said, "We need more rocks." He added more rocks to the drying art pages.

FIGURE 3.14 These photos show how learners authentically use materials from the natural environment.

As educators, we are challenged to be open to the variety of opportunities an outdoor environment can offer. We can bring learning materials like chalkboards, books, water tables and dress-up clothes outdoors, but are we open to seeing the natural materials in the outdoors and how they could be used to provoke inquiry? Our learners use many of these materials naturally and we can look to them for inspiration. Depending on where the outdoor space is, a connection to the neighbourhood and the world at large can be made.

THINQ

- What opportunities are there for outdoor learning around your school, other than recess?
- What are other kindergarten educators in your school and district doing in the area of outdoor education?

Inquiry in Action

Inquiry and exploring text forms

In Sue and Ann's class, Jenny brought in a worm house from home. She told the class all about it and how she built it. The students were very excited about building a class worm house. They decided to make a house in the empty aquarium that Ann had brought in. Sue, Ann and the children researched what a worm habitat needs and discussed this with Jenny, since she was the expert. As a class they worked together in the outdoor classroom to make the worm house. Everyone collected a worm for the house. Sue engaged small groups to create a shared procedural text on how to create a worm house. Sue and Ann observed learner participation in small group shared writing sessions and made anecdotal notes. They also observed and recorded how the children collaborated and shared responsibility to feed the worms daily.

How to build a worm house

Building a worm house

The chicken inquiry

Neighbours at the back of Antonella and Lori's school had chickens in their backyard. The children went to visit the chickens every time they were outside. They had many questions and wonderings about the chickens.

The educators began charting the wonderings and talked with the learners about what they might need for a chicken inquiry. The learners suggested books, feathers, styrofoam balls and real eggs. Over the length of the inquiry more wonderings were charted and questions were answered.

As it turned out, one of the children knew someone who worked at a local university in the biology department. The professor was invited to come and speak to the class where she shared a number of artifacts, answered many wonderings and provoked more questions. This was a great use of a knowledgeable other, and allowed learners to tap into the community and move their inquiry outside the four walls of the classroom.

The educators also contacted a farmer and the children hatched their own chicks from eggs the farmer gave them. The question of what the chickens do in the winter came up, which then led to an inquiry on hibernation.

This inquiry demonstrates that resources and materials to support student wonderings are all around us and come in many forms.

Some collected materials

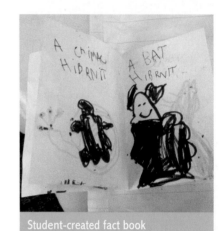
Student-created fact book on hibernation

What we know and want to know about chickens

Co-constructed knowledge about chickens

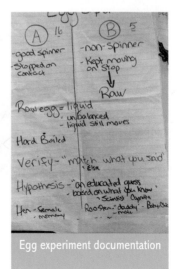
Egg experiment documentation

3.5 How does inquiry fit into the flow of the kindergarten day?

A question that frequently comes up is what inquiry looks like within the flow of a kindergarten day. Inquiry can be happening at any time, in multiple areas of the classroom and in a variety of learning domains. As educators we are called on to notice and name this learning and provide an environment that is conducive to this type of learning. The most effective way to do this is to have a plan that is adaptable and fluid. Large blocks of time with a limited number of transitions allow learners to engage with materials and make connections across learning areas.

Confirmation

Is it your experience that by allowing students to explore their interests, self-regulatory behaviour is strengthened? What do you think your colleagues would say?

Often we are bound by the structures and schedules in our schools. Sharing our knowledge of what is developmentally appropriate for young learners with other educators, administrators and parents will support inquiry. The flow of our day can also be disrupted by activities that need to get done. We know that for deep understanding to occur, learners need time to work through the process of inquiry.

Interruptions are a challenge to learners and learning. It is fitting that we keep in mind the questions, "Why this learning, at this time, for this child?" We should also consider the purpose of the experiences we offer, what we are learning about the child, and what the next steps might be. When children are fully engaged in and committed to an inquiry, purposeful learning occurs.

We need to negotiate our daily schedules to ensure that there is time for this type of learning. Slowing down and adapting a daily schedule for learner-initiated experiences and interests supports inquiry dispositions, skills and knowledge, and provides time for learners to make connections. It has been our experience that educator's daily plans change frequently when they are responsive to the learners. Educators observe, listen and document, and this is what drives the flow of the day.

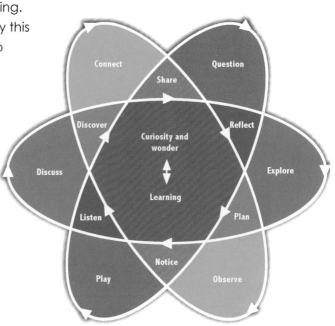

FIGURE 3.15 The flow of inquiry is non-linear and unpredictable. Our daily flow must accommodate this in order to maximize learning.

As mentioned in previous chapters, norms or procedures are vital to an environment that is negotiated and fluid. Co-creating a shared understanding of the norms that are applicable throughout the day is an important part of any classroom. This type of schedule works most effectively when self-regulating skills are explicitly taught and frequently modelled. The work of Shanker and Lewin-Benham indicates that when educators respond to and honour learners' voices and interests, and allow them to be responsible for their learning and that of others, self-regulation is nurtured and developed.

Reflective questions about an inquiry environment		
Space	**Time**	**Resources**
• Do indoor and outdoor spaces allow for differentiated instruction?	• Is our time used in a purposeful way that allows us to listen, observe and document thinking and learning?	• Do we offer a balance of open-ended materials for children to access during play?
• Is the space inclusive?		
• Has the environment been co-constructed with the children? Does it belong to them?	• Do we provide time and opportunity for students to make decisions and choices?	• Have we considered and chosen materials that reflect our children's real life contexts?
• Has the background been neutralized to focus on student learning?	• Is there time allowed for revisiting or extending an inquiry?	• Have the materials, resources and equipment been organized and labeled to ensure that children can access and put them away safely and easily? (E.g., use symbols, photo labels, and word labels to indicate where things go.)
• Could the space be de-cluttered?	• Does the flow of the day include a balance of teacher-initiated and child-initiated learning?	
• Do the children contribute to and co-construct what is on the walls?		
• Is student learning visible in the form of documentation and/or student-selected pieces?	• Do we ensure that there is sufficient time for children to get involved in inquiries in-depth, as well as time for them to organize their material?	• Are there a variety of materials and resources (familiar, novel, simple, complex)?
• Does wall space reflect the children's interests and inquiries?		
• Are visual displays at student eye level?	• Have we considered the attention span of our students so that the amount of verbal instruction suits the students' needs?	• Do learners contribute to inquiry materials?
• Is there a large gathering space for whole group discussions?		• Can materials be used for multiple purposes?
• Are there defined smaller gathering and quiet spaces for individuals?	• Is there time for daily classroom gatherings to share and reflect on inquiry learning?	• Do we use knowledgeable others as a resource for our inquiries?
• Can all children move in the space with ease?		

FIGURE 3.16 You can use these questions to reflect on your use of space, time and resources to support inquiry.

Revisit and reflect

In this chapter we looked at the environment as the context for learning. We explored the importance of examining our beliefs and values about children, relationships, learning and inquiry, and how these are reflected in our learning environment. This chapter provided examples of using anchor charts, class meetings, and knowledge-building circles to establish norms for an inquiry environment. We emphasized the importance of co-constructing space and materials with learners so they can take ownership of their environment. Using the outdoors for learning and ways educators can be creative about using natural materials was also explored. When educators make inquiry a priority for the classroom and share this understanding with other educators and the school community, then the significance of large blocks of time with minimal transitions for inquiry learning is made visible to all learners.

THINQ

• What new ideas do you have about creating a more inquiry-supportive environment?

• How could you use Reproducible 3A, *Considering educator values and the learning environment* and Reproducible 3B, *Reflective questions about an inquiry environment* to identify ways to create a more inquiry-supportive environment?

• Could you and your colleagues use Reproducible 3C, *Rethinking the learning environment* as the basis for a collaborative inquiry project?

• How could you and your colleagues make use of Reproducible 3D, *5 big ideas about inquiry and the learning environment*?

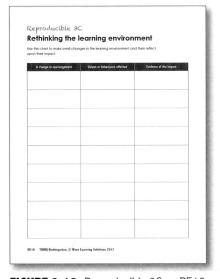

FIGURE 3.17 Reproducible 3B, p. RE9.   **FIGURE 3.18** Reproducible 3C, p. RE10.

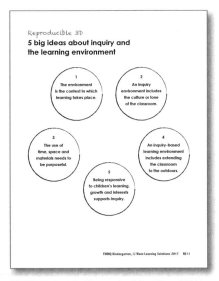

FIGURE 3.19 Reproducible 3D p. RE11.

Chapter 4

NEGOTIATING THE CURRICULUM:
Co-creating learning

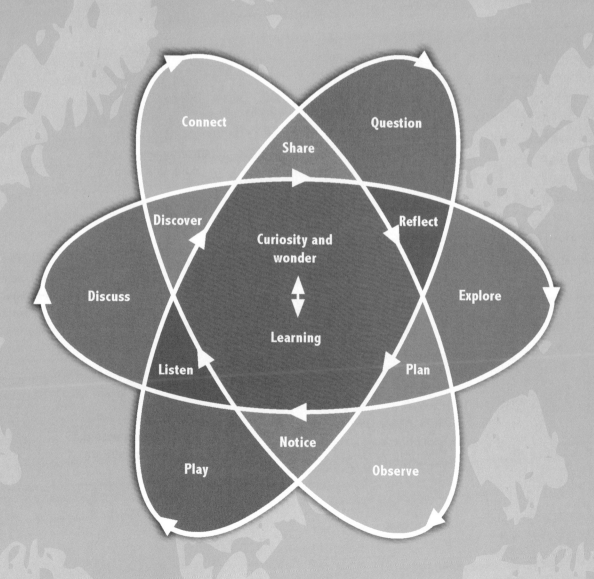

4.1 How do I "uncover" curriculum expectations through inquiry?

Big Idea
Inquiry learning and kindergarten expectations are complementary.

"If inquiry is non-linear and fluid, then how will I know when the expectations for learning are met?" "What does it mean to 'uncover' and 'negotiate' curriculum through inquiry and how do I do it?" "What is an emergent curriculum and how does it relate to a kindergarten program?" These are some of the questions that kindergarten educators face in an inquiry-based classroom and we will try to address them in this chapter.

Uncovering curriculum requires knowledge and understanding of kindergarten expectations, developmental stages, the child and their family. The process of uncovering begins with educators making learning visible: listening and observing, noticing and naming, and documenting a child's learning. This process is covered in more detail in Chapter 5. Educators can then map the observed and documented learning back onto kindergarten expectations, conceptual understandings and big ideas. In this way, educators can meet a child where they are in their learning. Together they can then set goals, determine next steps and co-create further learning. We look more closely at assessment for learning in Chapter 6.

Capacity
How confident are you in your ability to meet the expectations of curriculum in a learner-centred, inquiry-based classroom? What would like to learn more about?

Observe and listen to children's learning

Notice, name and document the learning

Map the learning onto the curriculum framework

Negotiate next steps in learning

FIGURE 4.1 Uncovering curriculum in inquiry means that educators observe and document learning, map it onto curriculum and use that understanding to negotiate next steps in learning.

4.2 What does it mean to "negotiate" the curriculum in inquiry?

In an inquiry-based kindergarten classroom, children are given the opportunity to collaborate with educators and negotiate their learning. Inquiry supports cooperation among educators and children. Together they negotiate the learning and the learning is responsive to children and their interests. Educators act as facilitators, creating opportunities for children to discover, dig deeper and construct new knowledge. Through inquiry, learning is authentic and based on real-life experiences.

When children are allowed to negotiate their curriculum, they are engaged and learn how to self-regulate. Educators create a culture of respect and responsibility, and encourage learners to choose topics for dialogue and learning. Children become more motivated, and all of this results in enhanced learning.

Food for Thought

"A negotiated approach means that curriculum is not solely emergent for the child or from the teacher but is negotiated — it is child initiated but teacher framed."

Murdoch and Le Mescam

THINQ

- How does the idea of a negotiated curriculum resonate with you?

- What concerns do you have about implementing a negotiated curriculum?

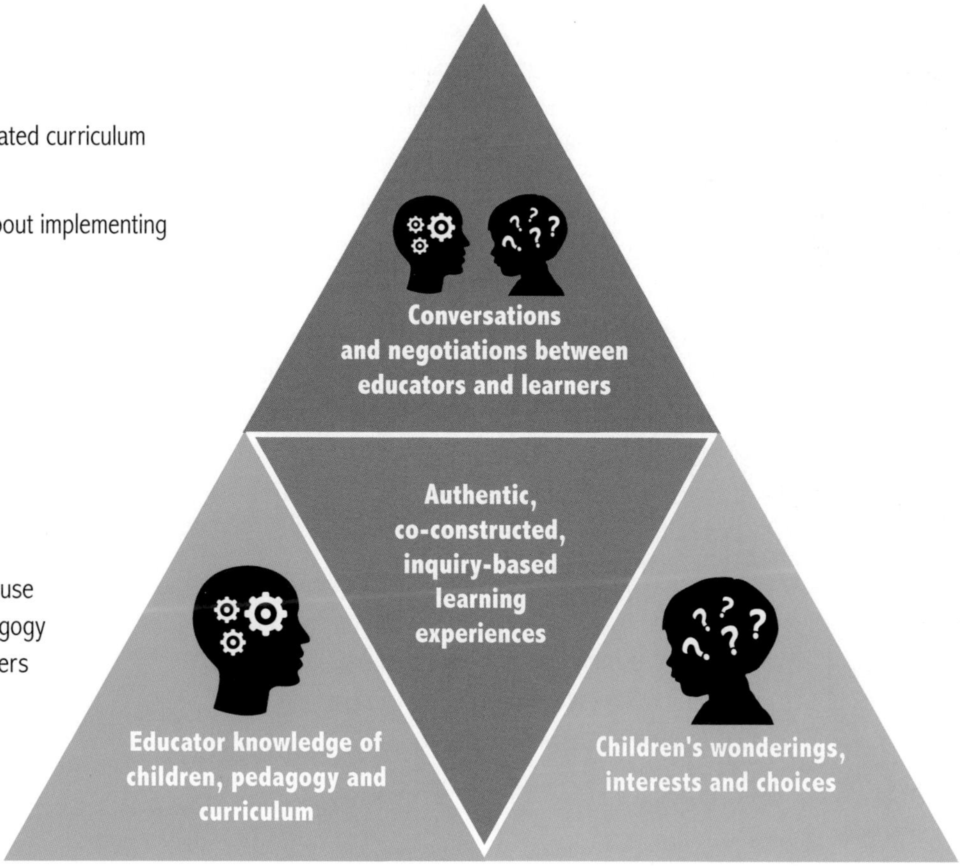

FIGURE 4.2 Negotiating the curriculum means that educators use their knowledge of children, pedagogy and curriculum to work with learners to co-create engaging, authentic and purposeful inquiries rooted in children's interests.

Conversations and negotiations between educators and learners

Authentic, co-constructed, inquiry-based learning experiences

Educator knowledge of children, pedagogy and curriculum

Children's wonderings, interests and choices

4.3 What should be "taught" in kindergarten?

Kindergarten is the introduction to formal schooling. As in grades 1 through 12, there are kindergarten outcomes, expectations, learning targets, conceptual understandings and/or content standards that are prescribed for all children. They answer the question "What should be taught?"

Standards-driven education

The purpose of curriculum is to ensure that all kindergarten children receive high-quality educational experiences. It is also intended to ensure equity of opportunity and reduce disparities in learning. Curriculum identifies the knowledge and skills children are expected to know and do, as well as the learner dispositions to be cultivated throughout kindergarten.

However, some researchers say that a standards-based curriculum is very prescriptive, and that expectations limit or narrow inquiry learning. They see curriculum as static and mechanical, highly controlled, based on an approach of direct instruction, and influenced by theories from behavioural psychology.

In their view, instruction aligned with curriculum requires that educators group children according to "type," which does not allow for individualized instruction. The role of the educator is that of a technician, administering the knowledge and skills necessary to be successful in kindergarten and beyond. Expectations require assessments that are standardized, not authentic, and limit the ways children can represent and demonstrate their learning.

Emergent curriculum

By contrast, in an emergent curriculum, children are contributing members of a learning community and their ideas are the foundation. The role of the educator in the emergent curriculum is that of researcher and practitioner. This approach to curriculum empowers children and educators. Collaboration in the school and community is valued.

Big Idea

In inquiry learning, kindergarten expectations answer the question "What should be taught?"

Capacity

In your classroom, how are the needs, abilities and interests of children balanced with the requirements of curriculum?

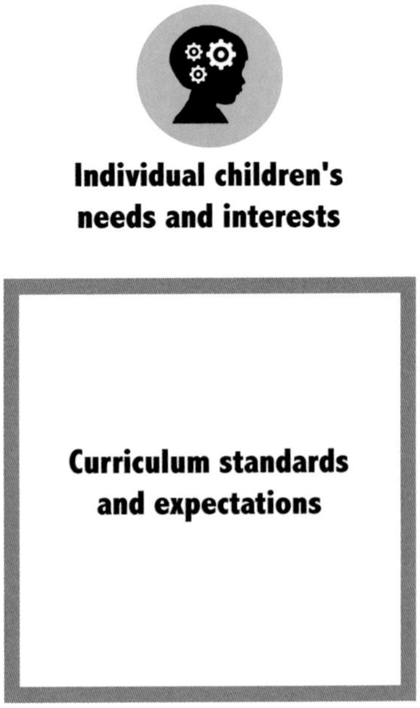

Individual children's needs and interests

Curriculum standards and expectations

FIGURE 4.3 Some educators worry that following a standards-driven curriculum leaves little or no room for the individual needs and interests of young learners.

The Reggio Emilia school in the Emilia region of Italy exemplifies an emergent curriculum approach to learning. There are no formal curriculum expectations; instead, teachers co-construct the curriculum with other teachers, children and parents. Children are considered architects and fabricators of values and culture. Children learn to represent their thoughts and ideas through the arts, which is regarded as an important form of language. The classroom environment is considered the third teacher. The Reggio Emilia school is highly regarded as an approach to learning for young children in the international education community.

Negotiated curriculum

In a negotiated curriculum model we can approach inquiry learning and the kindergarten expectations in a responsive manner. If we consider and implement a negotiated curriculum, we can take the positive, child-centred approach to learning that is exemplified in the emergent curriculum perspective and apply it to kindergarten. Our goals in this chapter are to demonstrate how to negotiate the kindergarten curriculum and how to view expectations as developmentally appropriate. We support the child travelling from one new learning experience to another, always mindful of the learning expectations, but never imposing one particular route to follow. Children move freely among the disciplines, investigating their questions of interest and concern, either alone or with the help of others. A negotiated curriculum is neither a standards-driven nor an emergent curriculum, but rather negotiated and co-constructed by educators and children, reinforcing a democratic approach to learning.

THINQ

- How convinced are you that curriculum expectations identify high standards and ensure equality of opportunity?
- What aspects of learning in your classroom are standards-driven, emergent or negotiated?
- How do we ensure that a curriculum is responsive when we follow the interests of the children in an inquiry?
- How do we ensure that we teach all the expectations when we follow children's interests?

Emergent curriculum based on the needs and interests of children

Curriculum standards and expectations

FIGURE 4.4 In a truly co-constructed emergent curriculum, there are no formal curriculum expectations.

Neogtiated curriculum

FIGURE 4.5 In an inquiry environment, negotiating curriculum can help balance and frame the needs and interests of children within the expectations of curriculum.

4.4 What is the role of the educator in a negotiated curriculum?

Educational psychologists John Dewey and Lev Vygotsky valued cooperation between child and educator, student collaboration, and the opportunity for students to participate in their own education. A negotiated curriculum allows a classroom to have all of these qualities.

In an inquiry classroom where the curriculum is negotiated, children are actively involved in curriculum discussions, voicing their opinions and having a say about their wonderings. Educators join in the conversations, and together they co-construct the learning. Educators map the learning onto curriculum expectations, big ideas and conceptual understandings.

The role of the educator in the inquiry classroom with a negotiated curriculum is that of an active listener, developing and maintaining a pedagogy of listening. Educators consciously and sincerely listen to and document students' thoughts, wonderings, anecdotes, reports and experiences. This may be planned or in-the-moment with the entire class, small groups or individual students. The educator becomes a co-learner and facilitator, framing the learning within the context of the curriculum.

Educators can invite students to participate in making decisions about what and how they will learn. This information can be used to create and inform the kindergarten program and environment. When educators take time to observe what motivates children, they are often astonished by the depth and breadth of children's interests and understandings.

Educators should notice and name the learning and regularly reflect and ask themselves: "What are these children sharing with me?" "How will this inform where we go next?" "How do I adapt the program?" These questions indicate a conscious, empowering pedagogy.

Big Idea
Negotiating the curriculum reinforces a democratic approach to learning.

Food for Thought

"Negotiating the curriculum means deliberately planning to invite students to contribute to, and to modify, the educational program, so that they will have a real investment in the learning journey and in the outcomes.

"Once teachers act upon the belief that students should share with them a commitment to the curriculum, negotiation will follow naturally, whether the set curriculum is traditional or progressive and whether the classroom is architecturally open or closed."

Boomer, Lester, Onore and Cooke

Capacity
How comfortable are you with implementing a negotiated curriculum in kindergarten?

The role of the child

A negotiated curriculum is a process through which students share authority in the inquiry classroom. Children are active participants in the decision-making of the inquiry classroom. They develop questions or wonderings about a topic that interests them. Children who are encouraged to contribute to their own learning when they are young become skilled in this process as they move through the school system. If we want our children to develop the dispositions of independence and responsibility, we must give them many opportunities to do so. Providing choice builds important decision-making skills and tells our children that we trust and respect them.

The learner's role in negotiating curriculum

In an inquiry classroom, educators provide opportunities for young children to make decisions and negotiate their learning. In addition to topics of interest, children are encouraged to make decisions about classroom routines and organization.

Saeeda noticed that the children had difficulty with the organization of the arts area of the classroom. Markers were often left with the lids off and crayons were in many different places in the classroom. In the past she would have imposed a rule about replacing markers and had the children comply. Instead she chose to encourage the dispositions of responsibility and respect. As a teacher-researcher, her wondering was: "How do I engage the learners in taking ownership for their learning tools?" She brought the children together.

Saeeda modelled her wondering with them by using a think-aloud. She said, "I am wondering why at the end of the day there are tools all over the place." She listened to their responses and rephrased some of things that they said. She shared with them that they were all part of the class community and how they should want to be respectful of each other and the tools in the classroom. They discussed how the use of the markers and crayons affected all of them. She was open to their suggestions about organization. Together, along with guidance from Saeeda about how to value everyone's opinions, the children decided they wanted to make a rainbow with their markers and crayons and organize them that way.

Saeeda provided containers and the children made a rainbow of colours, whether they were markers or crayons. Because they felt empowered, the children reminded and supported each other in the organization of the art tools from that point onwards. In addition, she had helped them to develop brainstorming skills, by allowing everyone to be heard and have an opinion without judgment.

After the decision was made by the class, Saeeda reflected on how it supported the children's self-regulation skills. She realized that she had modelled inquiry through her own wondering. The brainstorming skills that were endorsed supported future classroom discussions. She realized how negotiation had really moved the culture of the classroom to a more caring community of learners. It had helped to build a shared ownership and responsibility for the environment and create a more democratic approach to learning.

A negotiated solution

Bobsled inquiry

When we look at negotiated curriculum in a democratic culture, we see both educators and learners sharing decision-making and knowledge building together. Educators observe, question, engage, step back, brainstorm, give feedback and participate as co-learners. During the inquiry, educators also document student ideas, thinking and learning and then map this documented evidence onto curriculum expectations. The bobsled inquiry demonstrates this process in action.

1: The chart paper with bobsled or vet clinic

Mariella and Chris's class had two ideas for inquiry at the drama centre. While the educators were open to both ideas, the learners decided they wanted to vote on which one they should explore.

2: The little girl reading the book

After they decided on exploring bobsleds, the educators and learners realized they had many wonderings and needed to discover more. Both learners and educators brainstormed how they could find out more about bobsleds, including books and videos.

3: The class sitting on the carpet with teacher reading

Learners gathered in a variety of groupings to build knowledge about bobsleds and how to build one.

4 and 5: Boys drawing

The children determined that they need to draw designs for a bobsled. Those that were interested worked in pairs to create designs. All the designs were shared and designers explained their creations. The whole group negotiated which parts of each design they would use and gave their reasons why.

6: Kids measuring with ruler and 7: Child taping

Learners worked on a variety of jobs in creating the bobsled, including measuring and building. There were also painters, logo designers and engineers for the rope pulls.

8: Child pulling on ropes

The design team was very interested in was the rope-and-pulley system that is used in bobsleds. This learner demonstrates how it works in their bobsled.

9: Example of observational notes taken during the bobsled inquiry

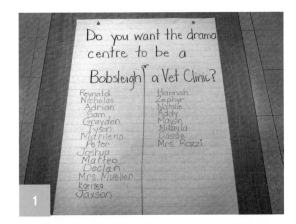

4

5

6

7

8

THINQ

• How might you have "negotiated" the bobsled inquiry?

9

Jan 21 Jon "if we use like a graph
we can find out which one
everyone will vote for"

Mari "it looks like bobsled has more, you
just have to count -1, 2, 3, 4 — 14

Z - what about vet clinic - can we do it
another time, can we still play animals?

Jan 23 Class discussion on building a bobsled
Looked @ books on parts of a bobsled
Many questions + wonderings - all seem
interested.
Greg - what would we used like to build it
do we need wood?

Ad - I think a cardboard box would be
good, we could paint it.

Kar - I wonder how to put it together.

Mar - What do you think we would need
should we make a list?

4.5 How do you build a negotiated curriculum?

Big Idea

The negotiated curriculum starts with the child.

A negotiated curriculum encourages children to contribute to, participate in, and transform a program, investing them in the learning journey and its results. This process may involve choice of ideas, planning future learning or selecting resources and materials. Educators invite students to navigate their learning journey by negotiating a curriculum around their expressed concerns.

In an inquiry classroom the educator understands many things: children and their individual learning needs; their families; developmental continua; and kindergarten expectations. The educator offers options and opportunities for children to explore their ideas. Observations and documentation help educators make informed decisions about individual, pair, small and large group instruction.

Since the negotiated curriculum starts with the child, observations play a critical role. When educators notice what and how children are learning, they are uncovering the children's thoughts, purposes, and understandings. In this way, everyone in kindergarten has a voice: children's curiosities are endorsed and respected, and educators can apply their expertise and experience. You may find Reproducible 4A, *Linking observations, learning and curriculum* to be a helpful tool.

Inquiry in Action

Framing learning within the context of curriculum

In Antonella and Lori's class, some of the children were interested in changing the drama centre into a dance studio. This supported a group of students' growing interest about dance.

The learners decided that they needed to name the dance studio. They came up with two names: the Butterfly Dance Studio and the Princess Dance Studio. They were not sure which one to choose. They approached the educators with the challenge they were having in deciding on the name.

The class had previously spent time on gathering information for graphing, so the educators asked the children the question, "What can we use when we want to collect information about what people are thinking?" One of the students said, "A graph of course!" The educators scribed the graph titles and the group asked those who were interested in the dance studio which name they preferred. Since it was almost a tie, the name became the Princess and Butterfly Dance Studio. This negotiation illustrates the benefits of coupling students' motivation with an educator's ability to frame it within the context of program expectations and prior knowledge.

The tally

The new name

How can I "cover" the curriculum and run an inquiry-based classroom?

A kindergarten educator, Jon, read about negotiated curriculum in the inquiry-based classroom and the many advantages it offered young children. He understood that a negotiated curriculum allowed children choice in their learning and he wanted to start the school year with the interests of the children, rather than just beginning with a strand in mathematics and language. He also wanted to trust the children to lead the learning and to have an understanding of their abilities.

However, he wondered how he would cover all the curriculum expectations. He questioned his ability to meet the diverse needs of the children and to provide the learning in the manner that would be appropriate for each child. He wanted to find out how to fulfill the curriculum and yet honour the interests of the young child. He wondered too, how he would be able to decipher the difference between a theme and an inquiry.

He had read the research about seeing the curriculum in a broad, rather than a narrow way. Before the children came, he reviewed the conceptual understandings of the kindergarten curriculum. In order to reference them, he printed them out and put them in a notebook close to his documentation. His fellow kindergarten teacher posted conceptual understandings on the walls at an adult level for reference, but he preferred a notebook.

He removed distractions from the classroom walls and prepared the environment so that the materials were open-ended. He took on the roles of researcher, active listener and documenter. He kept his iPad and notebook at his side. He understood that he was taking on the role of researcher. He was creating an inquiry about the inquiry approach to learning.

Jon noticed the children observing birds through their window, pecking at seeds on the ground. He listened to their conversations about what the birds were eating and what they were doing. He adopted an inquiry stance as they started to ask questions: "What are the birds eating? What kind of birds are they? How do birds fly? Why can't I fly? Where are the birds going in the winter? How will they know where to go? What will they eat in the winter?" Jon documented these questions so that he would be able to move the children forward in their learning.

Jon realized that he was learning alongside the children, which was a revelation, as he had previously not understood how as an educated adult he could be a co-learner with the children.

Jon reflected on his observations and started to map the kindergarten expectations onto the bird inquiry and considered how to be accountable for the expectations he was covering. He did two things: He went back to the curriculum expectations and identified those relevant to the bird inquiry on a chart. (See Reproducible 4A, *Linking observations, learning and curriculum*). He also started a photograph panel to identify the learning as it progressed. He posted photos and labeled the related conceptual understandings and expectations from the kindergarten program. Some educators call this an audit trail (see Chapter 5 for more information about audit trails).

THINQ

- How do Jon's wonderings reflect your own uncertainties?
- What kinds of questions might you ask the children after these observations?
- How would you support their learning moving forward?
- What other questions might you have about these children and their learning?
- How might you map the inquiry onto the kindergarten curriculum?

4.6 Who benefits from a negotiated curriculum?

When, in inquiry, the curriculum is negotiated, there are many advantages for the child, their family and educators. When educators build on the child's own questions, ideas, inquiries and wonderings about the world, they honour the child. Children are recognized as instrumental to their own learning. They learn responsibility as they become accountable for themselves. Children learn to self-regulate their learning. Their interest is sustained through choice of opportunities for learning in real-life situations. Children are enthusiastic and engaged in a program that is intentionally responsive to their interests and needs.

Families are respected through the ongoing communication between the school and home, particularly through documentation panels, learning boards, portfolios and other digital means. Educators honour the experiences that children bring from home and the information that parents provide to help move the learning forward. The families are partners in the learning.

Big Idea

There are many advantages for the child, their family and educators with a negotiated curriculum.

Food for Thought

"Negotiating the curriculum offers our best chance of maximizing the learning productivity of the classroom. The rule is simple. Learners will work harder and learn better, and what they learn will mean more to them, if they are discovering their own ideas, asking their own questions, and fighting hard to answer them for themselves. They must be educational decision-makers."

Boomer, Lester, Onore and Cooke

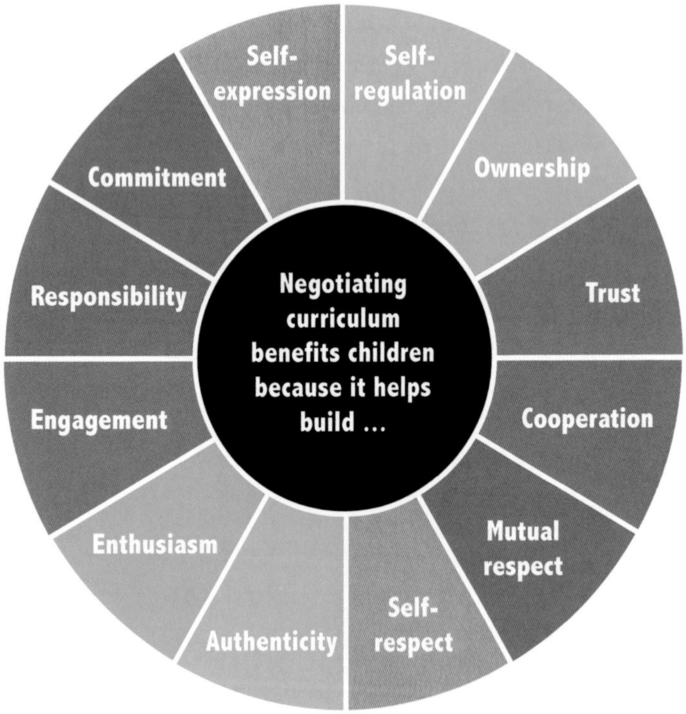

Negotiating curriculum benefits children because it helps build ...

Self-expression · Self-regulation · Ownership · Trust · Cooperation · Mutual respect · Self-respect · Authenticity · Enthusiasm · Engagement · Responsibility · Commitment

FIGURE 4.6 Allowing and encouraging children to direct their own learning through a negotiated curriculum builds the essential characteristics of confident and independent learners.

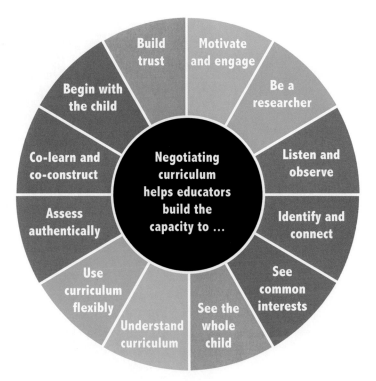

FIGURE 4.7 Negotiating, rather than directing learning requires that educators develop essential skills and understandings, which will ultimately benefit young learners.

THINQ

- How carefully do you listen to the children in your classroom?
- How is it possible to negotiate curriculum with children while still meeting the requirements of your school community and your administration?
- What are the greatest challenges you face in negotiating curriculum and what do you need to address them?

Conviction
How convinced are you that negotiating curriculum will generate meaningful benefits for learners and educators?

Inquiry in Action

Connecting inquiry to home and school

Josie and Antonella's class was wondering about snakes. One of their wonderings was which snake was the longest in the world. A number of the students thought the anaconda was the longest snake. They talked about the anaconda and learned that it was about 6 metres long. The class didn't really know how long 6 metres was, so Antonella and Josie had children lie down and asked them to estimate how many kids long it would be. They measured it on a long sheet of paper and cut out the snake so they could really see how long it was.

During the inquiry, Sara's mom let the educators know that one day after school Sara got home and took the vacuum out of the closet and stretched the hose out as long as she could. When her mom asked her what she was doing, Sara said she "wanted to see if it was as long as an anaconda." Sara's mom was thrilled that Sara was so excited about her learning that she would come home and take out the vacuum cleaner! When parents share how children make their learning visible at home, this adds another dimension to documentation and our understanding of the learner. This kind of reciprocal relationship benefits all: child, educator and family. When learners have choices and negotiate curriculum based on their ideas and theories, it is a great motivator for learning to spread to numerous contexts, including home.

Revisit and reflect

In this chapter we looked at the relationship between the kindergarten curriculum and inquiry. We shared the meaning of a negotiated curriculum as child-initiated but educator-framed. We explored the purpose of curriculum, which is to ensure that every kindergarten child has equal opportunities to learn certain skills and knowledge. We shared how the educator as a listener maps the children's interests onto conceptual understandings, big ideas and overall expectations. This chapter demonstrated how a curriculum that is negotiated and co-constructed with children through inquiry reinforces a democratic approach to learning.

THINQ

- How confident are you that inquiry and a negotiated curriculum can meet the needs of young children?

- How can we ensure that we uncover kindergarten expectations when we follow children's interests?

- In your classroom, what routines or organization could be negotiated, rather than imposed on children?

- How does your classroom reflect a democratic approach to learning? How could it be more democratic?

Big Ideas

4.1 Inquiry learning and kindergarten expectations are complementary.

4.2 A negotiated curriculum is child-initiated but educator-framed.

4.3 In inquiry learning, kindergarten expectations answer the question "What should be taught?"

4.4 Negotiating the curriculum reinforces a democratic approach to learning.

4.5 The negotiated curriculum starts with the child.

4.6 There are many advantages for the child, their family and educators with a negotiated curriculum.

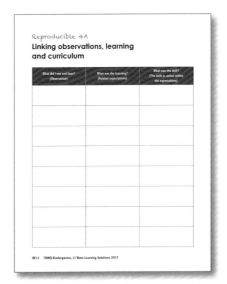

FIGURE 4.8 Reproducible 4A, p. RE12.

FIGURE 4.9 Reproducible 4B, p. RE13.

Chapter 5
DOCUMENTATION:
Making learning visible

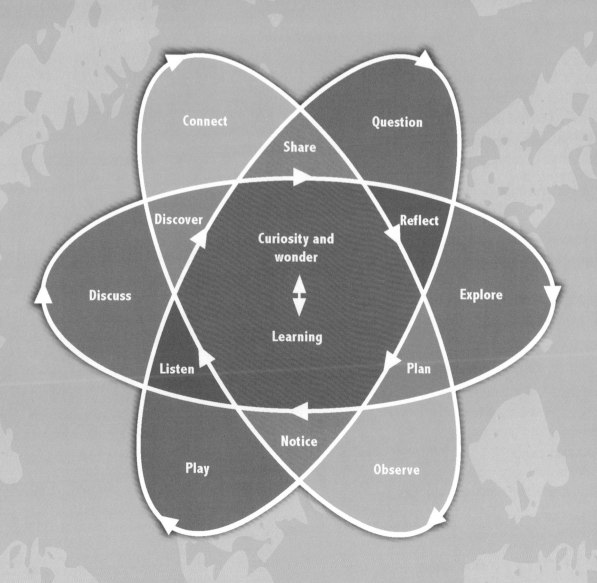

5.1 What is pedagogical documentation?

Documentation captures evidence of student learning and thinking, which can be gathered in the form of observations, conversations and representations. Pedagogical documentation refers to educators, children and parents studying the evidence and artifacts of student learning, analyzing it, and developing next steps to guide student learning. Carla Rinaldi (2001) refers to pedagogical documentation as "visible listening" — using artifacts that have been collected to reconstruct and revisit the progression of a child's learning.

Pedagogy is defined as both the understanding of how learning happens, and the philosophy and practice that support our understanding of learning. When educators look carefully at how learning happens, we become more attuned to what we do every day, reflect frequently on the purposefulness of our actions and understand how our actions affect children and families. What makes documentation pedagogical is the process of deconstructing and analyzing the documentation to make thinking and learning visible to educators, children and parents.

Sharing documentation with colleagues generates different perspectives and new questions about student thinking and learning. This is most effective when educators meet to describe and discuss collected documentation.

Educators can voice their own wonderings, examine their assumptions and judgments, and make informed and responsive decisions about the next step on the pathway.

Pedagogical documentation is an ongoing practice. The interpretation of evidence over time allows educators, children and parents to see a picture of longitudinal growth and development. It is not summative in nature, but rather, like inquiry: ongoing, generating new questions and insights as collected documentation grows.

Big Idea

Pedagogical documentation is analyzing evidence of thinking and learning in order to develop responsive next steps.

Context

How much of your documentation is pedagogical? How do you know?

Food for Thought

"Documentation provides a window on learning."

Helm, Beneke and Steinheimer

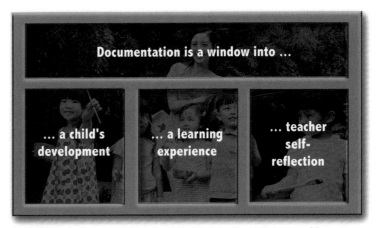

FIGURE 5.1 Documentation is a window into three elements of learning which, when taken together, support educator and learner decision-making about next steps in learning. Helm, Beneke and Steinheimer (2007).

Pedagogical documentation

Stefanie and Maria's class was finishing up an inquiry on space. Hunter entered the classroom and before he could even hang up his snowsuit, he approached Stefanie with a thought. She had her tablet in hand and recorded the conversation with Hunter. This is their transcribed conversation:

Hunter: Maybe after the space stuff we could wonder about the pyramids, like ancient Egypt, because I wonder about tombs.

Stefanie: You wonder about tombs?

Hunter: Yes.

Stefanie: Why do you wonder about tombs?

Hunter: Because I wonder how you get out of them…

Stefanie: Ok…

Hunter: And why there is mummies in tombs?

Stefanie: Do you know what a mummy is?

Hunter: Yeah, it's like a scary creature that sometimes lives in a haunted house for Halloween.

Stefanie: Ok, so you would like to investigate tombs and ancient Egypt?

Hunter: Yup.

Stefanie: Why are you wondering about this?

Hunter: Because I watched "Mr. Peabody" and there were tombs and I saw a mummy in it.

After documenting this conversation Stefanie shared it with Maria, her teaching partner. The team speculated that

Hunter chose from a collection of stationery at the writing centre to co-document his learning. The drawing shows his thinking about mummies and Maria scribed his words. Hunter drew ancient letters after his name.

Hunter had some feelings he needed to explore after seeing the movie.

The next day Maria took Hunter to the library and they found a number of books on ancient Egypt. Hunter read a number of the books and then shared his learning with the team and his classmates. Stefanie and Maria were hoping that Hunter's interest in ancient Egypt might spark a wider inquiry, but after researching mummies and sharing his thinking and learning in pictures and words, Hunter was good to go!

By capturing Hunter's wonderings through documentation and reflecting on it together, Maria and Stefanie were able to support Hunter's thinking and learning so that he could conduct a personal inquiry into his question. The recorded conversation and the artifact created and shared by Hunter are powerful pieces of documentation that can be revisited by the team, Hunter and his family.

THINQ

- Is there a purpose for documentation without reflection?
- What challenges are connected to pedagogical documentation?

5.2 Why document in an inquiry-based classroom?

Practicing documentation while engaged in inquiry allows educators to collect key evidence of learning, whether students are engaged in individual inquiries, like Hunter's mummy wonderings, or an inquiry that happens over time. By documenting over time and revisiting and reflecting on the documentation, a fulsome picture is gained of the wonderings, dissonance, collaboration, thinking and knowledge that are built throughout an inquiry.

One of the most powerful aspects of documentation is that it allows us to make visible those learning experiences that do not yield a product. Consider the following Inquiry in Action example; does this sound familiar to you?

Inquiry in Action

Invisible learning made visible

A kindergarten parent phoned her son's educator because she was concerned that her son was spending too much time "just playing" in class. In this particular case, her son and other children had been playing with dinosaurs and the mother pointed out that dinosaurs were not specifically mentioned in the kindergarten curriculum.

Documenting allows parents, learners and educators to see learning that may not be explicitly visible. In this play session, the children are learning to:

- build number concepts
- cooperate and collaborate
- problem solve
- expand oral language and vocabulary
- develop story sense
- refine fine motor skills
- create and follow a plan
- explore balance
- sort, select materials and construct structures

Exploring materials in multiple ways leads to learning in many areas.

THINQ

- What other learning might be happening through this activity?
- How does documentation assist us in noticing and naming the learning?

In addition to making thinking and learning visible, documentation is also important as a driver for extending inquiry-based learning. Gathered notes, photos, videos and products can point the way to next steps once interpreted and reflected on. When this documentation is shared back to learners, they can become partners in deciding and negotiating what the next steps in the inquiry might be and why. These are all critical aspects of inquiry-based learning.

Documentation also engages educators in asking questions of themselves and examining both their own practice and the inquiries that are happening in their environment: "Why is a child or group of children responding in this way?" "What are my thoughts about this child's learning?" "Is this learning purposeful?" "What big ideas or expectations is this tied to?" "What moves will I make next?" and "Do I need to rethink my approach?" Effective documentation allows for educator accountability and assists children and educators in finding meaning in what they do.

Simply put, through documentation all stakeholders can see and hear the thinking and learning that takes place during inquiry. We know that children have many ways to demonstrate skills and knowledge, and pedagogical documentation gives us the opportunity to capture all the varied ways learners make this visible. Student voice is seen and heard. Making the learning visible is the goal of daily documentation.

Confirmation

When have you used pedagogical documentation with inquiry? Was it effective? What were your challenges?

Food for Thought

"Documentation contains the 'presence of children' — their words, a piece of their work, some special object. In other words, it reveals more about the children than just their physical images."

Ann Lewin-Benham

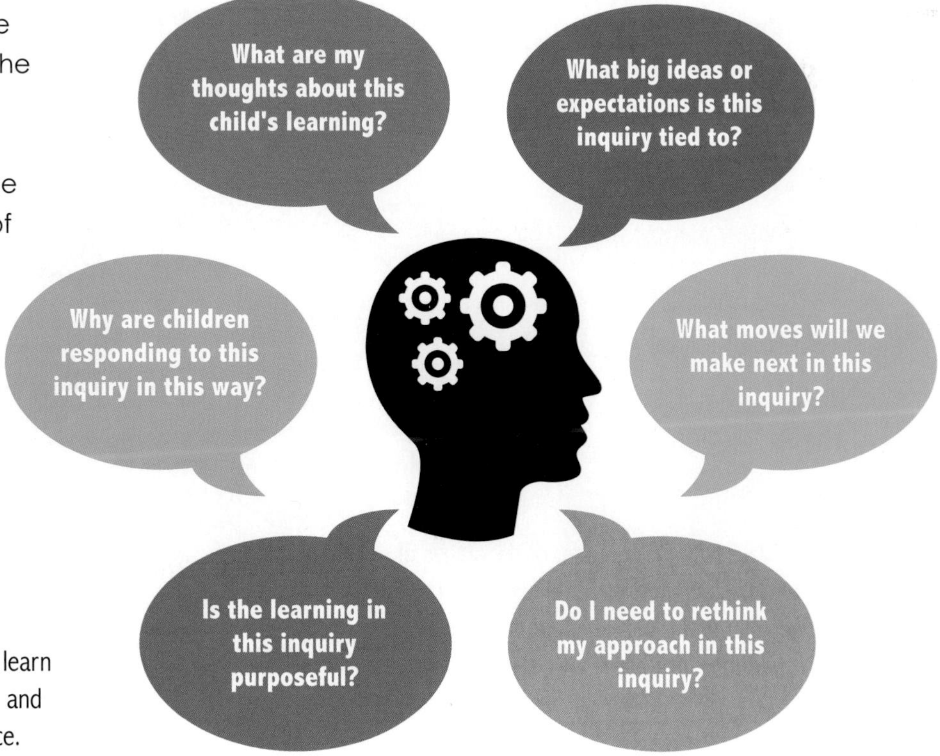

FIGURE 5.2 Pedagogical documentation is about more than recording events — it is a means to learn about how children think and learn, and how to improve instructional practice.

What are my thoughts about this child's learning?

What big ideas or expectations is this inquiry tied to?

Why are children responding to this inquiry in this way?

What moves will we make next in this inquiry?

Is the learning in this inquiry purposeful?

Do I need to rethink my approach in this inquiry?

5.3 Is there a process for documenting?

Observation is the core of an effective kindergarten program, but it is the documenting of these observations that guides us toward a deeper understanding of our learners' thinking and of the actions that we need to take next. Documentation in any form is a process that requires time and practice. Hilary Seitz (March 2008) identifies different stages that educators typically travel through as they become proficient with documenting learning and thinking. The table in Figure 5.4 is our adaptation of Seitz's stages.

Most kindergarten educators would be able to see themselves somewhere on this chart. Being aware of the stages of documentation assists us in knowing where we are and the knowledge we need to move forward with our documentation practice. We must also point out again that all documentation begins with listening and seeing. Observation is key to collecting purposeful evidence of thinking and learning. Slowed down, intentional observation is done with a stance of inquiry and curiosity so that we are open to seeing and hearing what is truly taking place. The authors of *Visible Learners* (2013) propose the observing is "the very heart of documentation."

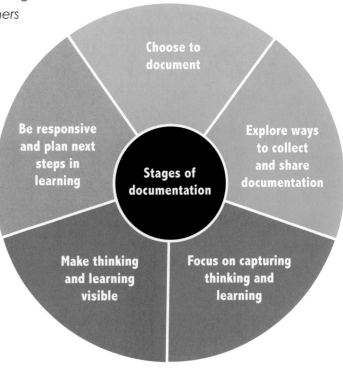

FIGURE 5.3 Being aware of the stages of documentation assists us in knowing where we are and the knowledge we need to move forward in our practice with documentation.

Stages of documentation	
Stages	**Characteristics**
Choosing to document	• Educators question what to document or where to begin. • Gathering may include many pieces of student work, rather than being selective. • Artifacts are educator-chosen. • Focus is on final products being displayed.
Exploring ways to collect and share documentation	• Educators practise, share and discuss collecting documentation. • Educators may use cameras, tablets, smartphones, apps or commercial products or programs. • Images are posted or displayed. • Slideshows are created and shared with children and parents.
Focusing on capturing thinking and learning	• Educators become more selective with what evidence they capture. • Less focus on product and more focus on the process of thinking and learning. • Children are included in choosing the artifacts to be shared. • Titles and captions are added to the artifacts that are shared.
Making thinking and learning visible	• Educators incorporate a variety of artifacts from multiple mediums to convey the story of children's thinking and learning. • Student voice is included in the documentation. • Contextual information is provided. • Connections are made with children's experiences to conceptual understandings and program expectations.
Being responsive and planning next steps in learning	• Educators revisit documentation to describe, analyze, interpret and reflect on it so that responsive decisions can be made about where the learning may go next. • Educators revisit documentation with students so that they are part of deciding next steps. • Documentation is used as a reflective tool for educators to examine and make changes to their practice.

FIGURE 5.4 Listening to and respecting what children ask and say is the most important thing educators can do to create powerful and relevant inquiry experiences for their learners.

THINQ

• Where do you see yourself in the stages of documentation?

• What might your next move be?

• When you examine your own documentation, how could you increase your focus on student thinking and learning?

How can we document learning?

The manner in which an educator documents learning should be one that is best suited for that educator. Documenters need to try a variety of methods before they find ones that suit their needs. Some questions to ponder when choosing a method for documenting are:

• Will the method of documentation make learning visible?

• Would the learning still be visible if we look again in the future?

• What are we trying to understand from our documentation?

• Is the documentation "meaty" enough to reflect on student thinking, feelings, interests, dispositions and behaviours?

• Is student voice evident in the documentation?

• Does the documentation promote further questions and wonderings about the learners and our own practice?

• If we share the documentation, will it engage other learners?

FIGURE 5.5 Choosing how to best document learning depends on the unique conditions and characteristics of you, your learners and your classroom.

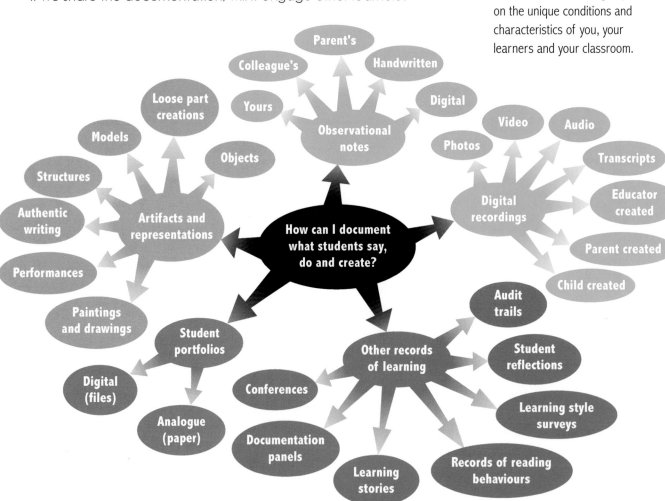

The habit of documenting

As with inquiry, educators are driven by a natural curiosity about their learners. When documentation and pedagogical documentation become an ingrained part of our practice, we can become more proficient at describing and interpreting student thinking and actions. Educators develop "new habits of mind in order to document" (Wien, Guyevsky and Berdoussis).

These habits would include determining which method of documentation works the best and having the required tools ready to go. It can be challenging to capture the moments you want if the notebook, sticky notes or electronic tablet are not at hand. Educators will also need to decide the audience for their documentation. When we look at the number of ways that documentation can happen, not all methods are for all audiences. Spending time with other educators and children revisiting documentation must also become a habit of mind. As we have mentioned, it is this revisiting and discussion that make the documentation more meaningful.

Food for Thought

"Documentation is not about what we do, but what we are searching for."

Carla Rinaldi

Documentation and inquiry

Educators, children and parents can travel through an inquiry using documentation as the map. The following Inquiry in Action looks at an inquiry in Mandy Sue's class. It is an excellent example of how documentation tells the story of the thinking and learning that began with a jar with worms. This collected documentation reveals that an engaging inquiry that is negotiated between educators and learners is a powerful vehicle for listening to children, collecting artifacts and understanding what children reveal. When we look back at this documentation it reflects the thought processes, theories, and thinking and learning of the children. It also sheds light on what the educators did as co-learners. The anecdotal notes along with the posted documentation make evident how the documentation affected the next steps Mandy Sue and her teaching partner took.

Educators Ask

What is an audit trail?

Audit trails were popularized by Dr. Vivian Vasquez, in her groundbreaking work with 3 to 5 year olds:

"An audit trail or learning wall, as my three to five year old students called it, is a public display of artifacts gathered together by a teacher and their students that represents their thinking about different issues and topics. This strategy is useful for creating spaces for students to re-visit, reread, analyze, and re-imagine various topics or issues. It is also a powerful tool for connecting past projects or areas of study to newer projects or areas of study. Further, it can be used as a tool for building curriculum as it visibly lays out the journey of the group's thinking and learning over a period of time."

Vivian Vasquez

The worm inquiry

This case study is an example of using multiple methods of documentation and creating a map of the inquiry to share with many audiences. The artifacts gathered include observations, scribed conversations and products that tell the story of the co-learning and knowledge building that occurred when learners proposed and tested their theories. Being able to view the journey informed the educators' and children's next steps.

Provocation

Mandy Sue has made a trail of student thinking and learning visible. The audit trail along with transcribed conversations with individuals and large and small groups shows the journey of an inquiry about worms. This inquiry was sparked by a provocation from one of her students who brought in a container with worms in it. She was very excited to show them off and talk about her experience. However, when she opened the container to dig out a worm, she noticed that they were not moving. "Oh no, I think they're dead!" Then she saw movement from one of the creatures and said, "Well at least my centipede is still alive!" The jar was passed around the learning circle and the other children observed and commented on why they thought the worms had not made it through the night:

- "They didn't get enough air."
- "They were too hot."
- "The container is too small."
- "The centipede ate the worms."
- "There's too much water in the container."
- "They drowned."

It is interesting to see how students built their ideas and theories from their co-learner's comments. One learner proposed that there was too much water in the container and another learner appeared to have agreed, but shared his thinking using different vocabulary. Mandy Sue and the learners brainstormed and charted what they thought a good worm environment would need. They also shared and charted their other wonderings. Mandy Sue also included what the children already knew about worms so connections could be made between prior and new learning.

Our wonderings chart

- How do they dig holes?
- Do worms hibernate?
- Do worms have bones?
- Where do they lay their eggs?
- How do worms stay warm and not get cold?
- Do worms have legs?
- Can worms climb?
- How do worms move?

Prior knowledge is gathered

- They help the garden grow.
- They love to be underground because they like to be cold.
- Worms don't have any bones.
- The bump on the worm pumps up when it eats food.
- Worms live in dirt.
- Spiders eat worms.
- Worms get eaten by birds.

The initial provocation of the worm jar and a trip outdoors to find worms were captured in photos.

Worm inquiry cont'd

Searching for worms

The learners only found a few worms in the back playground and one of the children suggested moving to the front. They found the soil to be softer and a few more wiggly friends were found. Mandy Sue made connections to stewardship in a class discussion about living creatures. The children talked about why worms are important and how they should be treated. This piece of the audit trail is powerful as it shows learners engaged in both the indoor and outdoor environments. This is reflected on the audit trail in text.

Mandy Sue and her students mixed the two types of dirt together and added it to the water table. Some students added their fruit peels to the mix, others added stones and sticks. Mandy Sue observed that these were some of the materials that the children had brainstormed when they were discussing. One child asked about the worms that had been collected the day before. Mandy Sue had put them outside and this caused many of the learners to question her motives to place them outside overnight. A child then explained that worms like the cold better and why. Mandy Sue observed that "light bulbs" lit up in several of the children as they thought about their own experiences with worms.

Investigating worms

Materials for investigation and building knowledge were used and/or placed in the environment. These included books, posters, magnifying glasses, videos, writing tools, measurement tools and small shovels. Learners built knowledge about worms in a variety of ways. Each day over the ten-day inquiry, student wonderings and discoveries were shared orally and on the expanding documentation trail.

Inquiry thinking made visible

- "The earth needs worms for digging and growing."
- "We need to be gentle with them."
- "The earth here is softer; it will be a good place for more worms."

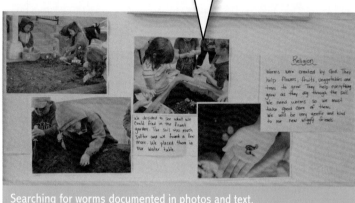

Searching for worms documented in photos and text.

Science, technology and measurement

- Connections are made to curriculum expectations.
- Images of students with books, student illustration and educator text about "that's the thing that makes the worm blow up."
- Materials are provided to build knowledge about worms and evidence of that knowledge is also shared.

Reflections and connections to stewardship gathered and shared in text.

Worm inquiry cont'd

Learners had already used balancing scales and rulers to measure and compare objects. Building on this prior knowledge, Mandy Sue provided similar materials for the children to measure and weigh the worms. Students first examined the worms (the lines, the ends, the saddle, the color, the size, etc.). Then they were invited to weigh their worm with a tool of their choice. One group attempted to balance the scale starting with two worms. The learners indicated that worms look about the same size but they seemed to weigh differently. Mandy Sue prompted the students by asking what other item they could put on the lighter side to try to balance the scale. The students experimented with another worm, a leaf, a twig and a linking cube.

After numerous attempts and rethinking, they found the leaf was the only thing that helped to balance the sides of the scale. The students then added worms to each side until it was balanced. They counted the worms on each side and ended up with five on one side and six on the other.

Reflecting on learning

During sharing sessions Mandy Sue prompted the children with questions about the findings and their wonderings:

- What new ideas do you have about worms?
- How did you measure your worm(s)?
- What tools did you use and why?
- Look at another friend's scrapbook. What did he/she do differently or the same as you?
- How did you use the scale? What comparisons with other items did you use?
- How long was your worm? Who had the longest and shortest worms? Who had worms of the same length?
- What other things could you measure using those tools?
- What items are the same length as your worm?

As the inquiry wound down, the students felt that the worms should go back to their garden. This was done with much ceremony and celebration!

Inquiry skills made visible
Estimating, predicting, questioning, planning, observing, rethinking, hypothesizing, representing, communicating and collaborating.

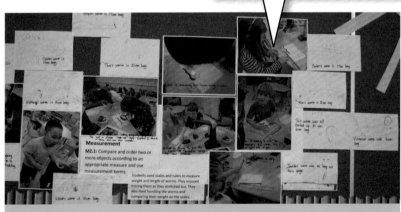
Photos of students measuring and weighing worms.

5.5 What does it mean for educators to be researchers?

Learning is the basic component of change. Educators as researchers are those whose practice includes reflecting on themselves as learners and how it affects the children they work with. As educators, when we examine and explore the thinking and learning of our children, we in turn are becoming researchers of our own practice. As Loris Malaguzzi points out, the two are dependent on one another: learning informs teaching, which informs learning. The definition of a researcher is one whose job it is to study a subject carefully in order to discover new information or understand the subject better.

The prefix "re" in research means "about" or "concerning." It implies searching repeatedly in order to figure out and understand. With respect to educators, the subject is both our learners and our own practice. Educators are challenged to see themselves not only as researchers of their students, but also of themselves and the impact and effectiveness of what they do every day in their classrooms.

Taking an inquiry stance to teaching

Research begins with a question or a wondering, just like inquiry. In fact, we believe that teaching is a part of the pedagogy of inquiry. We teach and co-negotiate curriculum, ideas, topics and wonderings. We build new knowledge and we begin making changes based on what we have learned. So when we refer to being in an inquiry stance, it is not just connected to what wonderings our learners have, but what wonderings we have about our learners and our own learning.

Carla Rinaldi believes that "when teachers make listening and documentation central to their practice they transform themselves into researchers." When we view and review our documentation wearing a researcher's cap, we are inquiring about: "What took place?" "What does it mean for this child?" "What does it mean for me as an educator?" "What might our next move be?" Pedagogical documentation is central to this research, especially when we engage with other educators and our children.

Big Idea
Reflective practitioners examine the link between teaching and learning and what their role is in this relationship.

Commitment
How committed are you to the idea of being a researcher into the effectiveness of your own practice? What are your greatest challenges in maintaining this commitment? How candid are you prepared to be?

Words Matter

Researcher
One whose job it is to study a subject carefully in order to discover new information or understand the subject better.

Protocols for documentation

Reflecting on and following protocols may support our research into what we see, hear and document about learners. Protocols are structured sets of guidelines or tools that are valuable in creating transparency and efficient communication, separating the practitioner from the practice, establishing a common language of inquiry, and allowing the focus to be on the learner and the learning.

FIGURE 5.6 Protocols can be helpful tools in negotiating a way through complex processes.

A protocol for documentation		
Step	**Description**	**Collaboration**

Study the documentation	**Focus: Describe the documentation**
	• Carefully study and describe the documentation.
	• Make notes:
	  • I saw …
	  • I heard …
		Review notes with colleagues, compare and contrast descriptions and observations.

Interpret the documentation	**Focus: Understand what it is telling you** • When I saw/heard … I thought … • The learning demonstrated was … • What does the documentation suggest about the child's thinking? • What are some questions we have? • What are our assumptions about the children and the learning? • What ideas and questions are children exploring? • How did my words/actions influence the experience? • Were there other influencing factors (e.g., other educators or children, environmental elements, shared learning, accommodations)? • What changes am I noticing over time and what do I do differently?	Share and discuss with colleagues. Be open to listening to all points of view and engaging in self-examination as well.
Consider implications for practice	**Focus: Apply what you learned** • What are the implications of this documentation for assessment for learning? • What are the implications of this documentation for my practice? • What further evidence of learning or information do I still need? • What types of additional documentation could provide this information? • Are students the focus of documentation and partners with me in the process? • What might be the next action for the child? • How might this information be used to plan for learning? • What does the evidence suggest to inform my pedagogical moves? • Where do we go next in the learning? • Why this learning, for this child, at this time? • What further professional learning do I need or want?	Share and discuss with colleagues. Be open to listening to all points of view and engaging in self-examination as well.

Having used this protocol with many educators, it is interesting that the most challenging step is the first one: simply describing what you see and hear. We are quick to go to interpretation or tie what we see and hear to a big idea or expectation. In fact, Katz and Dack (2013) have noted that "description is the one step that people tend to skip if left to their own devices." We have found that using this protocol when looking at documentation slows the process down and allows us to really listen to and see what is happening. Revisiting documentation for the purpose of pure description grants us the opportunity to listen and see again, which is what "re-searching" is about. It can be surprising what we miss the first time!

The interpretation step engages us in analyzing student thinking and learning, as well as our own practice. Many times when educators work through this protocol and revisit documentation, they realize that their questions could have been more open-ended, wait times could have been longer and that assumptions had been made.

The final step of the protocol allows us to research at another level. The prompts in this step focus on the implications of the collected evidence and educator interpretations. All of the steps of the protocol support research and inquiry as knowledge is constructed and more questions and wonderings are generated, not only about learners, but about educator practice as well.

As we discussed in Chapter 1, a characteristic of inquiry is dissonance. As researchers of thinking and learning, dissonance must be confronted and embraced. Edwards and Gandini have aptly named them "conceptual knots": questions we ask ourselves and others about the best way to move forward, when and what to observe, what to notice and name, or what something means. This can be messy work, but can gratifyingly lead to new knowledge about our practice. Researchers look at their subjects from every angle, and although cognitive dissonance may arise because of our research, ultimately both learners and educators grow and change.

THINQ

- Do you see yourself as a researcher?
- What dissonance might arise from interpreting documentation with colleagues?

> ### Capacity
> What do you feel are your strongest skills as a researcher? How could you become a better researcher? How might you go about doing that?

Food for Thought

"Learning and teaching should not stand on opposite banks and just watch the river flow by; instead, they should embark together on a journey down the water. Through an active, reciprocal exchange, teaching can strengthen learning and how to learn."

Loris Malaguzzi

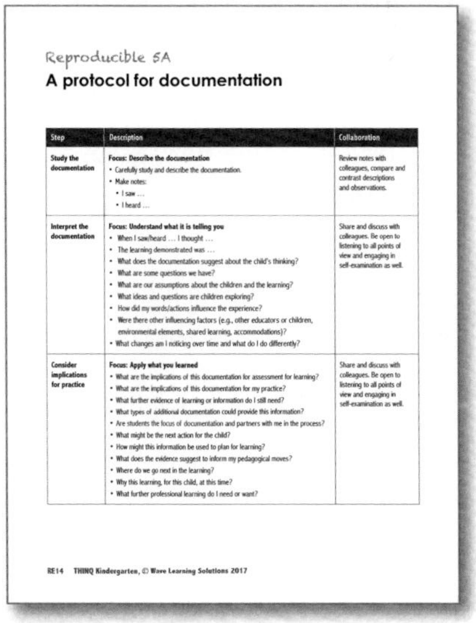

FIGURE 5.7 Reproducible 5A, p. RE14.

5.6 What is a child's role in documentation?

Big Idea

Young children can play an important role in documenting their own learning and the learning of others.

Context

What role do learners play in documentation in your classroom?

Diana and Amanda's class had started an inquiry about animal habitats. Some of the children were building a home for animals with large blocks. One of the children, Charlie, was observing what the other children were doing and commented to the educators that "the kids" were doing a good job. He went and got the classroom camera. He approached the builders and said, "Show me what you made," and proceeded to take a picture of the builders at work. When Diana asked Charlie why he took a picture he responded, "I took a picture so they can remember what they learned. When they make the home again they can use the pictures like instructions."

Diana and Amanda's classroom is a place where documentation was done with children, not to children. Our learners play an important role in documentation. As we have discussed, the purpose of documentation is to make thinking and learning visible to educators, students and parents. Part of this visibility is having students revisit documentation as well as taking a role in gathering the documentation like Charlie did. Modeling effective documentation practices and engaging our students in the practice allows them to revisit and rethink their learning, notice and name their thinking, model thinking for others, and plan next steps. In essence, they are engaging in assessment for and as learning.

Revisiting documentation

As Ann Lewin-Benham states, revisiting documentation "triggers reflective thinking." It engages learners in practicing metacognitive skills because it provides opportunity to think about and discuss their own thinking and thought processes.

There are any number of ways that students can revisit documentation. Many educators we have worked with establish a time within the day where photos, videos and artifacts are shared and discussed. This could be done in a variety of ways. Classrooms that are equipped with digital resources allow for screencasting or projection of videos and photos. Educators and students can choose pieces to share and intentional questions can assist learners in sharing their theories and the thinking that occurred. This type of sharing may require modelling and guided instruction to start, but students can

FIGURE 5.8 Young learners are often familiar and comfortable with technology.

become quite adept at it. Videos and photos can also be shared on tablets with smaller groups. Educators can print photos, have students describe what was happening and the actions they took, and include these scribed conversations with the photos. Audio recordings of students engaged in experiences are another way to capture thinking in order to revisit it. When children's scribed conversations are shared, student voice is validated and acts as an incentive for the additional sharing of thoughts.

These experiences allow educators to give new meaning to the traditional "show and tell" when students are showing and telling about their thinking and learning. It also gives educators opportunities to model the practice of noticing and naming thinking and learning, so that students can begin doing this on their own. This type of shared reflection is integral to inquiry as it provides a chance for participants to come together, confer about knowledge that has been built, discuss actions that have been taken, examine artifacts, and negotiate where the inquiry might go next.

Sharing documentation

Posting documentation in an accessible place is another way students can revisit their learning. Many of the educators we have collaborated with have a space in the environment where students can self-select products, photos and scribed conversations to be posted. Some educators call these Work Windows or Sharing Spaces. Each student has their own space to choose the artifacts they want to display. Students direct when artifacts are changed. These spaces are excellent springboards for conversations with students about the artifacts they choose to share and the context of the experiences attached to them.

Student portfolios, learning journals or binders that are accessible to learners are another way children can revisit their learning experiences. The artifacts gathered can be chosen by both learners and educators and offer ongoing, authentic evidence of thinking and learning. Documentation in these formats can also be accessible to families.

FIGURE 5.9 Examples of Work Windows. Leah and Eric have chosen what documentation to share.

FIGURE 5.10 Posted documentation shows both the voice of the educator and the voice of the learner.

When children look at their own portfolios or the portfolios of co-learners, they revisit experiences, rethink theories, reinforce new knowledge and get inspiration for new ideas and inquiries. When educators conference with children using documentation collected in this way, additional light is shed on knowledge that has been built or on misconceptions that need further examination.

Portfolios can also be digital. There are numerous apps and programs that support electronic portfolios. Students can become proficient at uploading photos and videos into portfolio files and opening them up to revisit artifacts.

Documentation displayed in documentation panels, learning stories, audit trails and annotated photos are also a method for learners to revisit experiences.

FIGURE 5.11 In Anita's class, documentation is displayed on cardboard boxes.

Revisiting documentation

Chris and Mariella created documentation boards about the inquiries in their class over the Christmas season. When the students came back in January, the boards were displayed in their shared learning centre. Chris and Mariella also included many of the books that were shared during that time. The educators gathered the children together to have a discussion about the boards. The learners were very excited about what they were viewing.

Mariella: "What do you notice about our shared learning centre?"

Alex: "There is a big board with lots of pictures (pointing to a photo) and I can see me!"

Mariella: "You are right Alex, that is you."

Other children started pointing and commenting that they could see themselves on the board as well.

Mariella: "Do you remember when we talked about the holiday season?"

One of the students started to recite a poem the class had learned. All the students joined in with lots of rhythm and expression. They chanted all four verses of the poem.

Mariella: "Wonderful, that's so amazing that you remembered that poem. I can tell you will never forget that one! We put together different pictures and words of what we did together. We would like you to come to the shared learning centre and look at the pictures and have a good talk about it. Maybe I might look at a picture and say, (pointing to some photos and scribed conversation) 'Hey Haley, do you remember the time when you and I measured the tree trunk and put it on the tree? We used the string and then we used the ruler…' and then we can have a conversation."

Nigel: "And even I can see me in that picture, I am working with my friends."

Mariella: "Great, you all sound like you are ready to talk about this with your friends."

Both Mariella and Chris spent time at the shared learning centre to observe and document the reflections and conversations that took place amongst the children. As they continued to use these boards, they found that they were made more powerful for revisiting and rethinking when students were a part of co-creating them.

Learners as documenters

As our learners see us documenting, they often model this by documenting their own learning or the learning of others. Our students are digital natives and are often well versed at using digital tools at a very young age! When we put these resources into our learner's hands, with instruction and support for those who require it, we have seen many children use them as documentation tools. Educators that we have worked with have commented that learners may go through some of the same stages of documentation that they do.

When children initially get a camera or tablet in hand, they photograph everything. With guidance and modelling they may become more selective and reflective about what they photograph. When children see a role for themselves in documentation, they become engaged in what videos, photos or products they want displayed or kept in a portfolio. We have often been in classrooms where children ask the educators to take a picture or video of an experience. In classrooms where learners felt comfortable with the tools of documentation, they will take photos and videos independently.

FIGURE 5.12 This learner documented the steps he took to make three groups of four.

The discussion that ensues is not only about what was captured but why the child decided to capture a particular moment or artifact. There are numerous apps and programs where children can use photos and audio to explain their thinking process. This can also be done with video. With modelling and guidance, learners can also scribe comments about their work digitally, or with handwritten text as in the images in Figure 5.13.

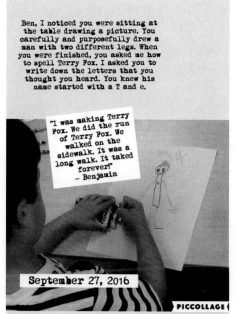

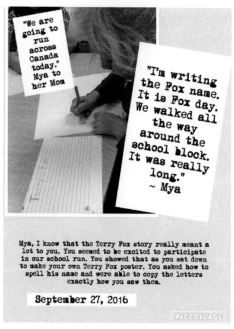

FIGURE 5.13 Frances documented learning by recording, and noticing and naming knowledge and skills. The children's voices are included as well, so that they are part of the documentation.

5.7 How do I use daily documentation to inform formal communications to families?

Educators we work with often wonder how they can use their documentation to inform families of their child's learning. They wonder how to use daily collections of observations for formal communications. So far in this chapter we have examined how documentation supports inquiry learning. Let's examine how we can use collected documentation to inform more formal communication with families.

When we prepare formal communications for families, we are moving from assessment *for* learning to assessment *of* learning. Documentation is the evidence of learning. The kindergarten program and its related expectations are the knowledge, processes and skills of learning. When we put the evidence (documentation) together with the expectations, we can then provide a fulsome description of the learning. Together, documentation and expectations provide a clear picture of each child's unique strengths, abilities and learning.

In the next Educators Ask, we share a sample of the documentation that educators have collected for Amelia. You will note that we have included some of the educator notes and artifacts that show Amelia's writing from the inquiry. This is not the entire collection of Amelia's documentation, but merely a sample to demonstrate how to prepare a formal communication from daily observations and documentation.

When educators prepare formal communications, they keep in mind the child, their family, collected evidence, expectations and stages of development. The educators who wrote the formal communication for Amelia's family used evidence as examples of her knowledge and skills from the expectations in the kindergarten program. This communication makes Amelia's demonstrated learning visible to her parents. As you read the formal communication, look for the evidence from the documentation. Then look for the expectations from the kindergarten program. Do you see the connection?

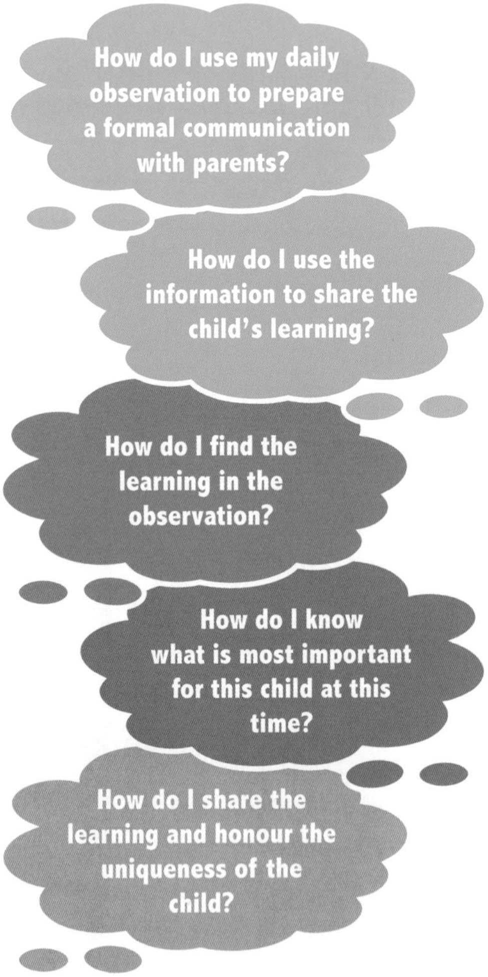

Capacity
How would you assess your own capacity and confidence in using documentation to communicate learning to families? What are your greatest challenges?

How do I use my daily observation to prepare a formal communication with parents?

How do I use the information to share the child's learning?

How do I find the learning in the observation?

How do I know what is most important for this child at this time?

How do I share the learning and honour the uniqueness of the child?

FIGURE 5.14 Many educators wonder about how to effectively use documentation to create formal communications with families.

How do I use documentation to create formal communication about learning?

We are often asked by educators about the connection between documentation and formal sharing and communicating. How do you use documentation to generate clear, valid and reliable descriptions of a child's learning?

The following case study presents some of the documentation of Amelia's learning and the formal communication educators generated based on their gathering and interpretation of their documentation.

Oct 20

- A. very interested in space book read during shared reading session.
- Lots of wonders about space to add to the wonder board.
- How did space get made? I wonder how the planets move? What are the planets that astronauts have gone to?

Oct 22–24

- Amelia went with small group to get books about space from the library; she also brought a book about planets from home.
- Spending lots of time with books and watching Storybot Outer Space videos.

  E: "What are you watching?"

  A: "That Story Bot video about planets. There are 2 other planets that are the same size as us."

  E: "Tell me about them."

  A: "Well Mercury is one and the other one I forget... wait... (A. uses the sliding rewind on the video to go back and listen to the song) oh yeah, it's Venus."

  E: "Can you tell me anything more about planets?"

  A: "The sun is in the middle and they go around it."

Oct 27

- I Wonder books set out at Space Place.
- A. used some environmental print.
- A. excited that we sang Sun song from video and is watching videos at home too.

Nov 1–3

- A. involved in building spaceship in classroom.
- Asked for silver paint for the boxes, had discussion about no silver paint and asked her what she could do. She asked S. to help her look up how to make silver paint online. She told us what she needed and the next day mixed the paint with J. and H. at the paint centre.

Nov 4–10

- A. brings in planet models that she made at home and shares them during knowledge building circle. Explains that she had lots of colours of plasticine at home so it "worked out good."
- Explains to class about the planets in the solar system and their names. Shows how Earth has blue and green plasticine bc it "has water and grass and dirt." Explains about ring around Saturn, that the ring is "rocks going around and around" and that "Jupiter is the biggest of all the planets."
- J., S. and R. share their knowledge too. M. asks if the sun moves too and all talk about it. Watch the video on the sun and it is confirmed the planets move but not the sun.
- Some kids want to build their own solar system.
- Over the next couple of days plasticine is placed at Space Place and models are built. A. sits at table and helps out with the rolling of the balls and talking about how many more they will need so they have all the planets.
- T. has the idea to name the planets and as a group they discuss the best way to do this. They ask for toothpicks and paper so they can label them. Amelia labels hers from home.

Formal communication for Amelia

Amelia is a learner who participates in all classroom experiences. She shows her skills in inquiry through her curiosity and her questions in oral and written form. We will continue to support Amelia's inquisitive nature by asking her questions about her wonderings.

Amelia shows her literacy behaviours when she writes questions and thoughts in her I Wonder Book, where she uses her knowledge of letters and sounds as well as locating print in the classroom. She demonstrates more literacy skills by using the classroom tablet for creating art pieces, writing stories with words and pictures, listening to stories, and watching videos for inquiries. She can practice reading strategies using the texts that interest her. These strategies would include introducing additional letters and sounds, continuing to use picture cues and using prior experiences to help with understanding.

Amelia showed leadership in the Space inquiry and assisted her classmates with their solar system models. When she is patient and listens to the ideas and thoughts of others, she shows us her ability to self-regulate.

Amelia understands concepts of measurement with non-standard units, uses the language of small, big and medium and displays this knowledge in a number of contexts. By planning and constructing our class spaceship she showed her knowledge of 2D shapes and 3D figures. Amelia has been working with numbers and can recognize numbers up to 5 in different combinations and count orally with objects to 22. Our next step will be introducing numbers to 10 as we continue to build on her understanding of counting and number sense.

THINQ

- How are your daily observations connected to formal communications?
- Do you see the connections to program expectations in the formal communication?
- Will parents be able to understand and support the learning at home?

Amelia's entry in her I Wonder book.

Amelia shares the solar system she created at home.

Labelled solar system created by learners.

5.8 What role can technology play in documentation?

Big Idea

Using technology can make documentation more effective and efficient.

Today, in our pockets and knapsacks, we carry the most amazing information and communication technologies. Handheld devices offer kindergarten educators powerful tools to make documentation and assessment more effective and efficient.

When kindergarten educators share with Emma's family "that Emma's inquiry skills are much improved," they are now able to give tangible evidence through photos or videos of Emma's learning, which have been gathered over time. This use of technology makes the learning real to families. The capacity of these devices to capture learning in-the-moment brings practical meaning to the concept of making learning visible. Not only is gathering evidence more effective, but pedagogical analysis and sharing can be enhanced as well. We can now review, reflect more deeply on, and share moments in learning.

Capacity

How can you use technology to make your documentation more effective and efficient? What can you learn from your colleagues in this regard?

FIGURE 5.15 Getting the most out of using technology for documentation requires forethought, collaboration and professional judgment.

Using technology for documentation and assessment

Stages	Key questions	Issues
Planning	• What learning can I best document with technology? • What learning might I be unable to document unless I use technology?	• Learner wonderings and interests • Curriculum expectations • Family needs and expectations
Gathering	• What devices and applications should we use and how and when will we use them? • What level of skill and understanding will I need, and whose advice could we seek? • What role might children play?	• Accessibility and reliability of devices • Educator expertise • Learner participation
Reflecting on learning	• How can I give feedback in-the-moment to learners? • How can we use it to better reflect on a child's learning? • How can we use it to reflect upon our own practice? • How can children use it to reflect on their own learning?	• Printing, posting and sharing • Classroom display • Learner access • Professional reflection
Communicating learning	• How can I use it to create a record of a child's learning? • How can I use it to better share a child's learning with their families?	• ePortfolios and storage • Sharing with colleagues • Family access

Revisit and reflect

In this chapter we looked at documentation and pedagogical documentation. We examined what it is and how it supports inquiry learning. We also explored the process and protocols of documentation. We shared the many ways that documentation can be done and how it can be shared with a variety of audiences. This chapter also looks at the important role that learners play in documenting and sharing their own thinking and learning.

THINQ

- What new documentation strategies and ideas from this chapter are you going to try in your classroom?

- Could you and your colleagues use Reproducible 5B, *28 ways to document learning* as the basis for a collaborative inquiry project about effective and efficient methods of documentation?

- With whom would you want to share Reproducible 5C, *8 big ideas about documentation and inquiry in kindergarten*?

Big Ideas

5.1 Pedagogical documentation is analyzing evidence of thinking and learning in order to develop responsive next steps.

5.2 Documentation is a tool to inform teaching and planning in inquiry-based learning.

5.3 Being aware of the stages of documentation assists us in knowing where we are and how to move forward.

5.4 There are as many ways to document as there are ways to learn.

5.5 Reflective practitioners examine the link between teaching and learning and what their role is in this relationship.

5.6 Young children can play an important role in documenting their own learning and the learning of others.

5.7 Documentation is the evidence of learning.

5.8 Using technology can make documentation more effective and efficient.

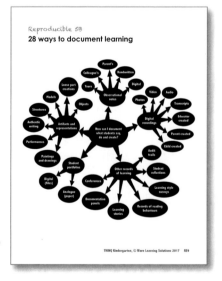

FIGURE 5.16 Reproducible 5B (p. RE15) and Reproducible 5C (p. RE16).

Chapter 6

INQUIRY ASSESSMENT IN KINDERGARTEN: Improving and sharing learning

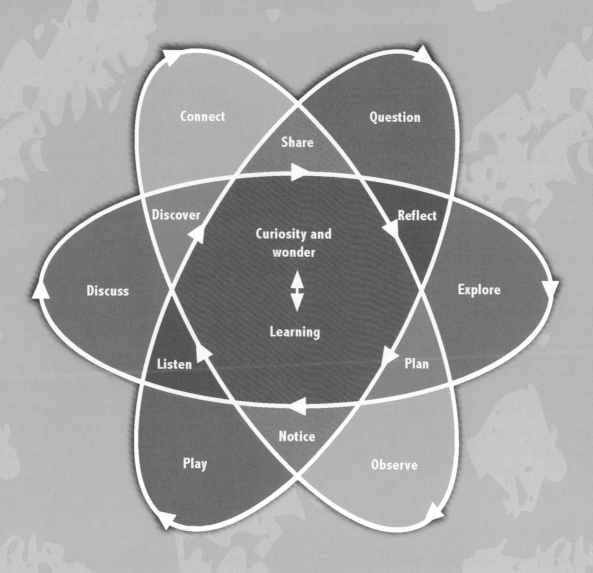

6.1 What is assessment in kindergarten?

Our assessment discussion begins by acknowledging that for many kindergarten educators, traditional notions of assessment focused on correct and incorrect answers, or passing and failing do not resonate. There is a concern that assessment is something that is done to children, not for children. Educators may feel that testing, scoring, measuring, weighing, categorizing, ranking, levelling or judging young learners is developmentally inappropriate, counterproductive and for some, even unethical.

Assessing young children

But can assessment be useful, constructive and positive for both educators and young learners? If we look at the meaning of the word "assessment," it comes from the Latin verb "assidere" which means "to sit beside." When we think of an educator sitting beside a child, it feels very natural.

When educators take an interest in what a child knows and can do, they have an understanding about that child's learning. When an educator sits beside a child, they gather evidence of that learning through documentation. Only in this way can the educator really determine where a child is in their learning, what they have learned, and where to go next.

When we come to this understanding of assessment in the kindergarten classroom, we realize that assessment is a way to support learning for a young child. It is a part of our everyday way of being in the classroom. Assessment is a way of listening to each individual child and giving educators confidence and certainty that they are supporting young learners appropriately and fairly.

Food for Thought

"Assessment always performs functions other than the ones teachers and examiners normally think about and take account of... It is an act of communication about what we value."

David Boud

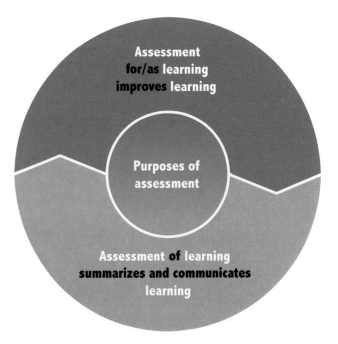

FIGURE 6.1 Assessment supports young learners by helping educators understand a child's learning, how best to improve it, and how to summarize and communicate their achievement and growth.

6.2 How do you assess inquiry in kindergarten?

Big Idea

Young learners can grow and develop as inquiry thinkers.

If inquiry "needs to happen from the very start" (Jerome Harste), then kindergarten educators need to think about the inquiry skills and abilities of their learners.

The processes and skills of an inquiry stance are the core of inquiry and assessment. Inquiry is as varied and unique as each classroom and learner, but the processes and skills remain constant. We have identified six essential inquiry abilities — these are components of the kindergarten program expectations. Educators keep them in mind as they observe and assess young children in inquiry.

Questioning

Questioning is the ability to pose questions and to state wonderings in different contexts and for different reasons. Young learners can ask questions about their world: "Why does the sun shine in that window every morning?" "Where does the rain come from?" They can ask questions about their problems and about how to solve their problems: "Can you help me make a colour of paint to match the bird?" "How can I move my building without it falling?" They can ask questions to clarify their understanding of a situation: "What are you doing with that board?" "Where are you going with that water?" In kindergarten, educators encourage, welcome and invite children's questions and use them to drive inquiry. This gives voice to learners' questions.

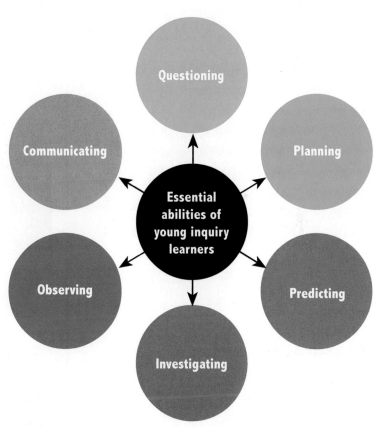

FIGURE 6.2 You can use the framework of the six essential inquiry abilities to help notice, name, improve and communicate the inquiry thinking and processes of young learners.

Planning

In kindergarten, planning is the ability to think about organizing in order to meet a goal. It is about the ability to identify actions to meet an outcome: "We will need to feed the fish every day so it doesn't die." It is about making logical connections: "I mixed these two colours together and made another colour." It is about selecting and using materials to carry out an exploration: "If we get a big piece of paper and markers, we can make a road for our cars. My Grandma bought me one for my cars."

Predicting

Predicting invites children to construct a hypothesis or theory about the outcome of a situation. They are able to identify cause and effect with events that happen repeatedly, as well as to recognize patterns of events: "Hey, there is a puddle of water under my boots. The snow keeps melting when I come in." Children can make and describe connections and generalize between different matters, incidents and experiences: "It happens with the snow on my boots and the water on my frozen gloves." They can transfer rules from one situation to another: "What would happen if we brought a snowman inside?"

Investigating

Investigating is the process of finding all of the details or facts about something in order to discover who or what caused it or how it happened. It may include research through books, smartphones or tablets, or it may involve brainstorming with other children. It is an organized way of finding a response to an inquiry as well as a structured way to approach exploration.

The ice gloves

These inquiry learners demonstrated all of their abilities in this inquiry: they made observations and asked questions about snow and ice; made predictions about freezing water; planned an experiment; and investigated and observed the results, all while communicating with educators and with each other.

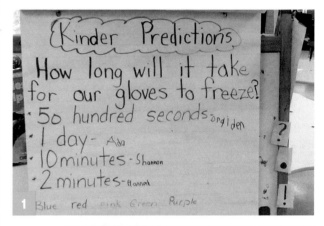

Young learners are able to evaluate a situation and then re-adjust their approach based on their experience. For example, when a kindergarten class was creating a garden, they did research about light and soil. They had a class discussion about what seeds to plant and created a map for the seeds. They made a chart about watering the plants as a shared writing experience. Together, they investigated gardens before creating their own.

Observing

Observing refers to the ability of young children to attend to things in their environment. It is the ability to use their senses to gather information and includes the ability to attend to details. Their attention becomes more focused as they spend longer periods of time in observation. Children are able to name and describe things that they have observed: "I saw the caterpillar move across the sidewalk. When I looked through the magnifying glass I saw it had lots of hairy things and the different colours on its back. I want to paint a picture of it so I can show my sister."

Communicating

When children communicate, they have the ability to present their ideas to others through various methods. It may be through retelling or explaining their discoveries. It may be writing about their journey. It could be through photos, a learning story or picture panel. The arts are viewed as a method of communication, such as drawing, painting, modelling, music or movement. It may be through mathematical processes such as graphs, surveys or charts. Educators can support children through direct instruction with the various ways of communicating about inquiries.

Assessment of the six processes and abilities of inquiry is consistent with our beliefs about curriculum and inquiry. It reflects a child's progress towards the attainment of curriculum outcomes outlined in various kindergarten programs.

Conviction
Are you convinced that kindergarten children can and should be developing their inquiry abilities and that you can help them do it?

Capacity
As a co-learner, how well do you currently model and reflect on your inquiry abilities with your learners? How could you be more effective?

Context
What are the inquiry abilities of learners in your classroom? What can they do and what could be developed further?

THINQ

• What view of assessment for the early years resonates for you?

• How is the value, purpose and use of assessment in your classroom different from what we have described here?

• How closely do our six essential inquiry abilities align with your ideas about inquiry in kindergarten?

6.3 What is the role of assessment for learning during inquiry?

Big Idea

Assessment for learning is fundamental for improving inquiry learning.

Assessment for learning improves learning. When educators use assessment for learning, they determine where the learners are in their learning, where they need to go, and how best to get there. Assessment for learning is not a tool: it is a shift in thinking about what matters in schools. It moves the focus from categorizing students to students' learning.

Confirmation

What is your experience with assessment for learning? Have you observed any benefits for young learners?

Over and over again, research studies have demonstrated that when formative assessment is well-implemented in the classroom, it can improve student learning. Assessment is a powerful catalyst for learning. Formative assessment can produce huge gains in students' achievement, and is sufficiently vigorous that educators can use it in diverse ways and still get great results with their students.

As children are wondering, investigating, exploring and researching, both educators and children are engaged in reflecting upon information from dialogue, demonstration and observation. They are responding with ideas and feedback that are immediate and directed at learning, in real time.

Observation and documentation are the keys to assessment for learning in an inquiry-based kindergarten. In kindergarten, assessment for learning is part of everyday teaching in everyday classrooms. Assessment for learning occurs in real time. Not only is information about learning generated, but also it has the positive effect on the inquiry learner. The learner becomes engaged and motivated to learn.

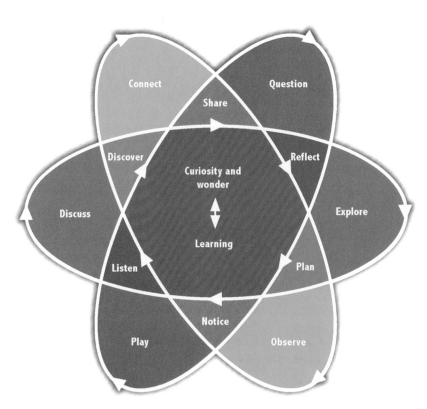

FIGURE 6.3 As children and educators cycle back and forth through the inquiry process, assessment for learning is focused on understanding and maximizing learning.

6.4 What is "noticing and naming the learning"?

"Noticing and naming the learning" is an assessment strategy, a form of descriptive feedback. When we notice and name the learning, we provide an image or description of the learning taking place and make it visible to the young child. As children participate in and reflect on inquiry experiences, noticing and naming the learning helps them develop and deepen their understanding of what their learning looks like.

A feedback-rich environment is built on reciprocity. If the child is given an opportunity to notice and name the learning with other learners, this opportunity allows the child to both share in the learning and to reflect on their own learning, and also to assess their own learning and that of their peers. Noticing and naming the learning supports and fosters children's growth and helps them learn the language and skills of assessment. This allows young learners to practice metacognition.

In conjunction with clear and shared learning goals, assessment for learning allows children to be partners in the assessment conversation. They can notice and name the learning for themselves and others, after it has been modelled by educators.

As a form of feedback, noticing and naming the learning offers educators many opportunities to: (1) make thinking and learning visible, (2) consolidate learning, (3) build metacognitive skills (through reflection), (4) show growth in learning and (5) identify for educators and children where to go next in the learning. Figure 6.5 on the next page provides examples for the different purposes of noticing and naming the learning.

Capacity

What are the challenges you face in noticing and naming learning?

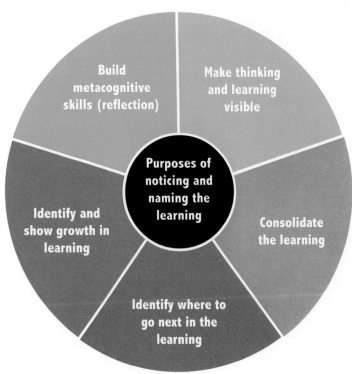

FIGURE 6.4 Noticing and naming learning makes learning visible to both educators and children, and is a key assessment strategy in kindergarten classrooms.

Examples of noticing and naming inquiry learning

Purpose	Description	Inquiry example
Make inquiry thinking and learning visible	Noticing and naming inquiry learning.	"You were really thinking about how to measure the weight of the minerals. I noticed that you used a scale and balanced the rock with four blocks." Jonathan said, "Hey Devon, you should come over and tell me what happened with the snow."
Consolidate the learning from inquiry	Noticing and naming learning from an inquiry to help consolidate and make explicit what knowledge and skills have been constructed.	Educators wanted children to become familiar with mathematical language. To consolidate mathematical thinking, they took a more open approach (i.e., a stance) to listening for indications of children's understanding of a mathematical concept. They observed children in their inquiry and listened to their conversations during routines as well as ongoing mathematical discussions. Educators noticed and named the mathematics language and concepts so that the children's learning was made explicit. They also consolidated the mathematical language in different contexts: "I saw that you made a snowflake with two sides that are the same. We call that symmetry in mathematics."
Build metacognitive skills through reflection	Noticing and naming the learning in order to make inquiry thinking visible and to help children reflect on what was done and why.	Two children were playing with small blocks and a toy car on a large piece of paper. An educator observed them drawing roads and making buildings with blocks. All of this was done using non-verbal communication. Educators made a video of the interaction and then watched it with each other and with the children. They noticed and named what they saw with the children and asked questions to make their metacognitive skills explicit — their planning, their organization, their reflection and their next steps: "We saw that you had one car, some blocks and a large sheet of paper that you were drawing on. What was your plan? What will you do next?"
Show growth in learning through the inquiry	Noticing and naming the learning to help with application of learning from the inquiry.	Educators added a variety of rocks, stones and found objects to support the children's inquiry about minerals. They documented how and why the children used specialized vocabulary with the rocks and minerals. The educators noticed and named the vocabulary. The children also begin to notice and name with each other: "This mineral is a crystal." "Your rock is hard but my crystal is harder and could break it."
Identify where the inquiry should go next	Noticing and naming the learning in order to focus on new opportunities to extend the inquiry and the learning.	Educators were documenting a group of children writing about their outdoor inquiry in puddles. They were familiar with the expectations in the curriculum and stages of writing, and were able to notice and name the writing strategies the children were using. "Tyrone, I noticed that you were writing about the puddles. I saw that you were trying to write a word. Where can you find that word in the classroom?" They used that information to make decisions about where to go next in the learning and co-created a word wall so children could find common words. They introduced dictionaries and showed the children how to use them and where to go for help with unknown words.

FIGURE 6.5 Educators and learners can both notice and name learning, use it to make learning visible, and then extend and improve it.

Noticing and naming the learning

Kelly had initiated an inquiry around patterns with her new kindergarten class. She watched Reese, who was putting beads on string in a pattern.

Kelly: "Tell me about your learning, Reese."

Reese: "I am making a bracelet."

Kelly: "What are you learning about your bracelet?"

Reese: "I am making a bracelet for my mom."

Kelly realized that Reese had little background with noticing and naming the learning and being a reflective learner. Reese kept referring back to the activity of making a bracelet. Kelly rephrased her question to notice and name the learning.

Kelly: "Reese, I notice that you are putting beads on a bracelet. I notice that you have two red beads and one blue bead and then two red beads and one blue bead. We call that a pattern. A pattern is when you repeat a design over and over. Have you heard of patterns before?"

Reese nodded her head in a "yes" response.

Kelly: "You made a pattern with colours. Tell me about your pattern."

Reese: "I made two red beads and one blue bead and two red beads and one blue bead and two red beads."

Kelly: "You are learning about patterns. Did you know that you can also make a pattern with size with big and little beads? Do you see someone making a pattern with big and little beads?"

Kelly extended Reese's learning by identifying other patterns at the table and challenged her to use size or shape. By noticing and naming the learning, Kelly was able to share the language of mathematics with Reese and extend her learning.

Context

What kinds of conversations do you have with your students about their learning? When and how often do you have them?

Food for Thought

"My observation is that when children build relationships of mutual trust and respect with adults, and those adults engage them regularly in meaningful dialogue, the children develop reciprocal expectations in regard to dialogue."

Brenda Fyfe

"Through our noticing and naming language, children learn the significant features of the world, themselves, and others. These understandings influence how they treat each other and their environment."

Peter Johnston

THINQ

- How could you make noticing and naming a greater part of your everyday practice?
- What are the greatest challenges you face in noticing and naming learning?

6.5 How do you construct learning goals in an inquiry-driven classroom?

We are often asked whether it's realistic to have a learning goal for an authentic inquiry that starts with the interests of young children and has no predictable outcome. "Inquiry learning goal" feels like an oxymoron to some educators. They ask, "Don't learning goals limit inquiry learning?" and "How do I make learning goals developmentally appropriate for young children?" We believe that yes, learning goals can and should be used for inquiry.

Creating learning goals

When educators ask themselves, "How will students in this kindergarten class be different as a result of this inquiry?" they have the basis for learning goals. Learning goals are crafted from the expectations, conceptual understandings and big ideas in the kindergarten curriculum. Learning goals describe what knowledge, skills, thinking, engagement and behaviour we expect from kindergarten children.

As educators engage with children in inquiry-based learning activities, they draw on their observations of the children and their knowledge of the overall expectations and big ideas in the kindergarten curriculum to develop learning goals.

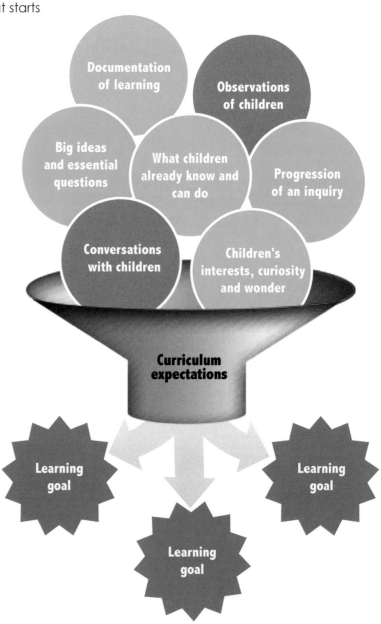

FIGURE 6.6 Learning goals are shaped by many factors. They represent the knowledge, skills, abilities and dispositions that children develop based on curriculum expectations.

Learning goals help children think about and begin to direct their own learning by making what they are learning "visible" to themselves. Learning goals are stated in terms of what children understand and what they will be able to do. Learning goals may apply not only to an individual situation (short term) but also to an entire year of learning (long term). These are abilities, skills, dispositions, inclinations, sensibilities, values and knowledge children develop based on the kindergarten expectations. They are developmentally appropriate so that every child, no matter their stage of development, can enter the learning.

Sample learning goals

Here are some examples of long term learning goals and related short term goals.

I am learning...

... to explore the world around me.
... to recognize the people in my community.
... that materials can be sticky, fuzzy, hard or soft.

... to ask questions about my world.
... to ask for directions.
... to ask for help when I need it.

... to express my ideas in different ways.
... to use pictures to tell a story.
... to use puppets to tell a story.

... to understand numbers.
... to know which number is more and which is less.
... to match numbers to pictures.

... to explore new ways of doing things.
... to tell a story with my body.
... to show my feelings through music.

FIGURE 6.7 Short term goals set interim milestones in support of the attainment of long term learning goals.

Inquiry in Action

Applying learning goals

When Sasha and Simone designed their learning environment, they combined a careful examination of the kindergarten expectations with their observations and authentic conversations with children about what interested them and their thinking. They realized that in order to identify the valued learning that children might exhibit through their play or in inquiry, they required a good understanding of all these elements.

They also realized that if they initially kept the learning goals broad (i.e., based on overall expectations), they could more easily keep these goals in mind, so that they would be ready to respond to the wide array of learning that might emerge during children's play. The words and phrases they used in conversation with children came from the learning goal that the educators identified in their planning.

One of the broad learning goals was "Learning about the world through inquiry." The educators thought that the learning might look like children wondering, asking questions, observing, and making predictions. They used this language when they spoke with children and began to notice and name their learning. Emmett was experimenting with building blocks, appearing to be trying to build a taller tower. After observing Emmett for some time, this was part of the co-authored conversation:

Simone: "Hey Emmett, tell me about what you are doing right now."

Emmett: "My tower for this city keeps falling over."

Simone: "Do you have any ideas for a solution?"

Emmett: "Well maybe if I put more blocks at the bottom, kind of like a base, it won't fall over."

Simone: "That's an interesting prediction. Try it out. Let's see what happens."

More and more, we see that the conversations educators have with children are rich opportunities to discover what they are thinking and learning, and that how we approach these interactions is critical.

Communicating goals

Learning goals are communicated in many different ways with kindergarten children. Learning goals can be written, shared verbally, illustrated with pictures, clarified through documentation, and introduced by noticing and naming the learning. Learning goals often are shared in the moment, in real time as the learning occurs. Some learning goals are shared with the children verbally after observation of a child or a group. Some learning goals are shared in conversations with individuals or small groups prior to an inquiry. Other learning goals and success criteria are co-constructed on bulletin boards, documentation panels or learning boards. Children can illustrate learning goals through photos or drawings. When children reflect on the learning goals and success criteria daily, they internalize the learning and can name it for themselves and their peers.

In addition, a common understanding, or even the co-creation of the success criteria for learning goals, allows children to be partners in the assessment conversation. They can notice and name the learning for themselves and others, after it has been modelled by the educators.

Inquiry in Action

Co-constructing success criteria

In September, students asked Tim and Wei about what they were going to learn that year. Tim and Wei shared a learning goal and co-constructed some criteria for learning for the year with the children and wrote the class's thinking on a chart.

Goal: I am learning.

Criteria from the children:
- I can wonder
- I can look at books
- I can write my name
- I can ask questions

Later that day, the educators asked some children to use the iPad and take photos of other children learning in the classroom. Tim and Wei printed some of the photos and together with the children, considered the actions in the photos and how they were reflected in the learning criteria that the class had developed. When they asked the children to place photos near the criteria that they illustrated, the children noticed that they needed to add more criteria. They added:

- I can build
- I can plan
- I can guess

As time progressed, the children added more criteria and wanted to create new learning boards. With support from the educators, who were referring back to the kindergarten expectations, they organized the chart into more specific learning goals and more explicit criteria:

- I can find information
- I can share my thinking
- I can listen to the ideas of others

Not all learning goals were produced into charts or boards as the educators responded to the children's inquiries and interests. The educators were conscious about placing the criteria around the learning goal so that there was no sequence to the learning. In this way every child could see themselves in the learning, no matter their developmental level.

Goals as identities

Another way of sharing learning goals in kindergarten is through identities, such as "I am a writer" or "I am a painter." When learning goals are communicated as an identity, children build a sense of being and an understanding of their own character. They learn to understand their own abilities, potential, and to then take responsibility for their own learning and become self-regulated learners.

Within the community of kindergarten learners, educators and children negotiate and come to a common understanding of what these identities entail. When the learning goal is an identity, then the criteria or elements of the identities can be developed using the language of the children. In this way, children can identify with the learning, no matter their developmental level, and everyone can see themselves as a learner.

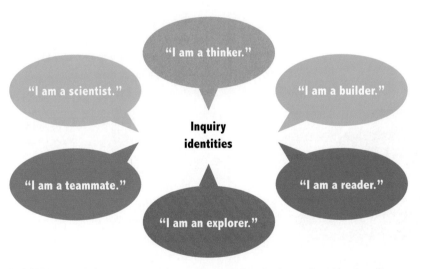

FIGURE 6.8 When learning goals are presented in the form of an identity, all children can identify with the learning, whatever their level of development.

THINQ

• Are you familiar with learning goals as identities? How do they support children's learning about themselves?

• How do you notice and name when you have shared learning goals in your own practice?

Inquiry in Action

Inquiry identities

Greyson was a kindergarten student at the early stages of literacy development. The educator, Lindsay, wanted to know if he identified as a writer.

Lindsay: "Are you a writer?"

Greyson: "No, I am a boy."

They looked out the window together. It was raining.

Lindsay: "Can you paint the rain, Greyson?"

Greyson picked up the paint brush and started to make strokes on the paint easel with a brush.

Greyson: "I painted the rain."

Lindsay: "Can you make the letters of your name?"

Greyson: "I can make a 'G' 'R' 'E' 'Y' 'S' 'O' and 'N'," he said, as he printed his name on the painting.

Lindsay: "Let's go look at the learning board. This board says 'I am writer.' Do you see what the children are doing in the photos? Do you see Maya painting a picture? Do you see Boston writing his name? Can you do these things, Greyson?"

Greyson nodded his head.

Greyson: "I am a boy and I am a writer. Can we take a picture of my painting and put it on the learning board? I am a writer."

6.6 What is the relationship between documentation and assessment of inquiry?

Carla Rinaldi makes the case for documentation as the "genesis" of assessment. She believes that in the process of documentation, educators "make the element of value, as well as the indicators you have applied, visible and sharable." In addition, she argues that "from your documentation, the children can understand not only their processes but what you value as meaningful for their learning processes."

Pedagogical documentation is the journey that educators, children and parents take when they revisit evidence or artifacts of student inquiry in order to analyze and interpret ongoing thinking and learning and guide next steps. Documentation provides an authentic account of a student's learning and it shows accountability when planning and communicating each student's progress.

Commitment
Are you prepared to be a researcher as you gather documentation to deepen learning, guide instruction and co-construct next steps in learning?

Food for Thought

"As the teacher and students revisit the content of the documentation, the learning process is also made visible to the students, allowing them to assess their knowledge building process while interacting with others."

Martine Pellerin

"Documentation reveals a child's theories about the world, their social reactions, the role they play within a group. It uncovers the path of learning and makes it visible to the outside world. With this information teachers are able to reflect on how the learning is proceeding, they can sense what resources or materials might further the children's investigations."

Fraser

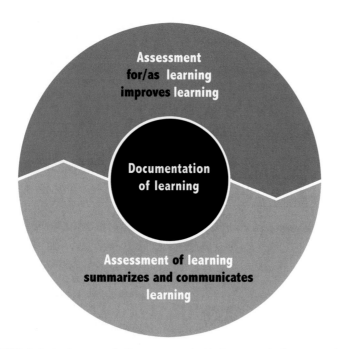

FIGURE 6.9 At the core of all assessment in kindergarten is documentation of the evidence and artifacts of children's learning.

Evidence of learning

Documentation is the primary way to gather evidence of learning. Ongoing collection and interpretation of evidence of learning assists educators, children and parents in seeing a picture of growth and development over time. The understanding of a child's knowledge and skills is captured through listening, observing and having conversations, which are all elements of documentation. Daily observations may be both planned and spontaneous in inquiry. When educators document, they are mindful of many things, such as their knowledge of each child, developmental levels, unlocking children's thinking, feedback, the curriculum, the learning environment, pedagogical content knowledge, and learning theory.

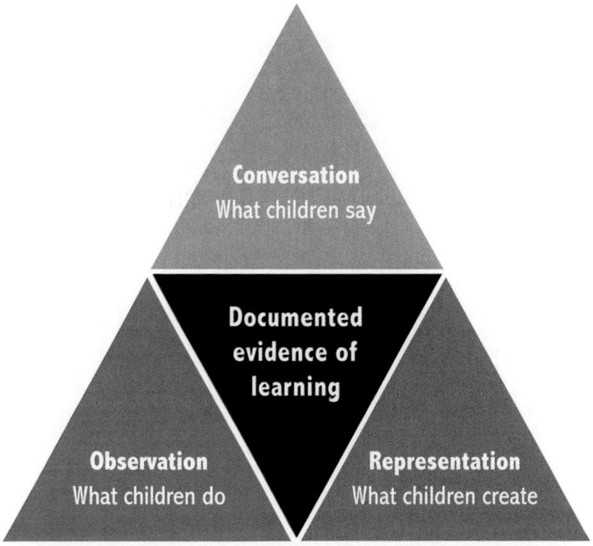

Uses of documentation

Documentation serves different assessment purposes in the inquiry classroom. When educators as researchers reflect on the documentation, they have an opportunity to determine whether their pedagogy has been effective and where to go next in instruction. Documentation also allows educators to determine what children are learning and whether they have demonstrated growth in relation to goals and expectations.

When educators and children reflect on the documentation together, it allows them to notice and name the learning and co-plan goals on where to go next in the learning. Children are then also able to self-assess and assess the learning of their peers. Figure 6.11 provides examples of the different ways of using documentation.

FIGURE 6.10 Effective documentation requires gathering a balance of evidence from observations, conversations and children's representation of their learning.

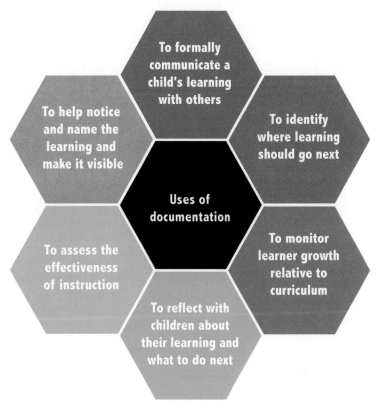

FIGURE 6.11 The value of documentation should be measured not by how much evidence is collected, but by the degree to which it helps improve, summarize and communicate children's learning.

6.7 How can I communicate learning to families?

When we talk to parents of kindergarten children, they tell us that they want educators to truly know their child. Parents want to know if their child is meeting kindergarten expectations. It is the responsibility of the kindergarten educator to frequently communicate each child's learning to their parents in a meaningful way. Parents are a child's first teacher. It is important to value what families know about their child's interests, preferences and ways of learning as part of inquiry learning.

Sharing documentation with families

Communication with families about the class's inquiry learning can take many different forms. It is important to know and understand your community so that you can share information about inquiry in the most meaningful manner to them. Some families visit the classroom regularly and see the documentation and learning panels that display inquiry learning. Some families prefer that displays are shared through technology. There are personal communication books, portfolios and documentation photo books that can be shared with families. You will decide the best way to create and maintain ongoing communication based on your conversations with families and your relationships with the community.

Documentation shows the progression of growth in an individual child's development during a period of inquiry learning. Looking at photos, videos and samples of children's products reveal patterns of growth and change over time. Educators, children and parents can travel through an inquiry using documentation as the map. Documentation allows educators and parents to focus on what a child is able to do and to appreciate their growth through an asset lens.

Big Idea

Ongoing communication with families about learning in the inquiry classroom is vital to the home-school relationship.

Commitment

Are you committed to ongoing communication with parents? What do you find most challenging in this regard?

Educators Ask

Past, present and future

Many educators tell us they sometimes feel caught between a rock and a hard place: while education reform is seeking to design a system for the decades ahead, educators live in the present, and sometimes with parents who remember the system from decades ago. The conceptual gap can be many decades, perhaps even more, given that students today will still be part of the global workforce 50 years from now.

This is a major communications challenge that shouldn't be underestimated. There are no easy answers but it makes transparency, openness and dialogue with families essential for helping to identify, understand and close the gap.

You can read more about this challenge in *Preparing for a Renaissance in Assessment* by Peter Hill and Michael Barber.

Formal reporting

Educators are required to formally report to parents about a child's progress with respect to the kindergarten program expectations. Formal reports are one way of communicating with families. It is essential to use examples from documentation and portfolios to illustrate the learning in the context of the kindergarten expectations.

When educators share their documentation and evaluation of a child's learning with parents, along with co-constructed next steps, then they have moved to an assessment for learning stance.

THINQ

- What does ongoing communication with families look like in your practice?
- What are your challenges with ongoing communication with families?

Inquiry in Action

Haydn's story

Haydn's parents were hesitant to enrol their son in an inquiry-based kindergarten program. Haydn was a young kindergarten child. He expressed himself with only a few words and had little experience playing with other children. His parents wondered if the inquiry program could meet his needs.

The educators kept continuous communications with Haydn's parents by phone, notes and email to apprise them of Haydn's progress throughout the fall. When preparing the formal written communication, the educators knew Haydn, his parents, the kindergarten expectations and the developmental stages. Keeping this in mind, they prepared the following formal written report from their ongoing documentation:

> Initially upon entry to the class, Haydn would wait for help and stand quietly watching other children. He then would go play by himself, often with the shells that he had carried to school in his pockets. Now he follows morning routines independently and plays with a few friends.

> At first Haydn would communicate with others using gestures. Now he shows growth in his oral language by speaking in simple sentences, especially with his friends.

> Through his curiosity in shells, Haydn demonstrated literacy and mathematics behaviours, inquiry skills, language development, and social skills. After books about shells were introduced to Haydn, he then chose similar books by himself. He sorted shells by size, length and colour, and used language modelled by others. His friends joined him in his shell investigation; they used a magnifying glass to have a closer look.

> Haydn's interests in natural materials will be used to support his language development by modeling words and sentences. We are working to extend his mathematical behaviours by sorting and patterning beads, blocks, and natural objects. Haydn's play with his friends is being encouraged and we will continue to notice and name his progress in this area.

At the interview the educators held with the parents, it was shared that the progress that Haydn was experiencing at school was also visible at home. His parents had a better understanding of the value of the inquiry-based program for Haydn's growth in learning. The parents looked for ways to support Haydn's learning goals at home.

Revisit and reflect

In this chapter we looked at inquiry assessment for young learners, why it is important and how to think about children as inquiry learners. We also explored why assessment for learning is so fundamental to inquiry-based teaching and learning. Noticing and naming the learning in conjunction with well-constructed learning goals and documentation of learning are essential for:

- understanding children's inquiry learning,

- reflecting on the effectiveness of our practice,

- making learning visible to children, and

- identifying next steps and opportunities for learning.

Lastly, we considered the importance of and ways to communicate with families about what inquiry is, why it is important and ways to do it.

THINQ

- What in this chapter has altered your ideas about assessment for kindergarten learners, what it is, its value and purpose, and how it should work?

- How could you and your colleagues make use of Reproducible 6A, *Purposeful planning for inquiry assessment in kindergarten*?

- Which of your colleagues might find Reproducible 6B, *7 big ideas about inquiry assessment in kindergarten* clarifying or informative?

Big Ideas

6.1 Assessment is part of our everyday practice with young children.

6.2 Young learners can grow and develop as inquiry thinkers.

6.3 Assessment for learning is fundamental for improving inquiry learning.

6.4 Noticing and naming the learning makes learning visible to educators and learners.

6.5 Learning goals help co-learners to notice and name the learning.

6.6 Documentation provides an authentic account of a student's learning.

6.7 Ongoing communication with families about learning in the inquiry classroom is vital to the home-school relationship.

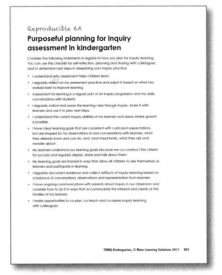

FIGURE 6.12 Reproducible 6A, p. RE17.

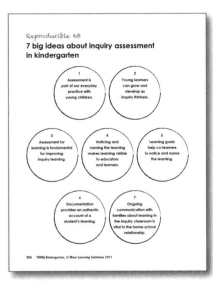

FIGURE 6.13 Reproducible 6B, p. RE18.

Chapter 7

THE HEART OF INQUIRY IN KINDERGARTEN: What matters most

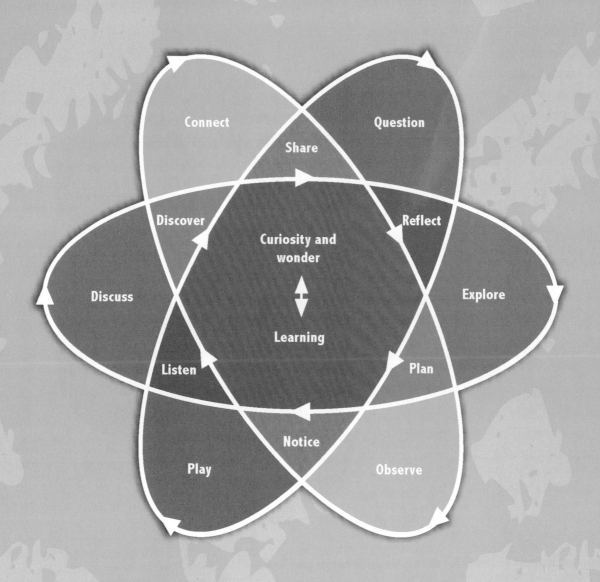

7.1 What lies at the heart of inquiry in kindergarten?

Throughout *THINQ Kindergarten* we have presented and discussed what we feel are the qualities of successful kindergarten inquiry. We have also endeavoured to deliver practical suggestions for planning, learning and assessment that are meaningful, relevant and doable for classroom educators. Regardless, inquiry, by its very nature, can seem a complicated thing.

In this last chapter we want to talk about what matters most by highlighting six key points that we believe are at the heart of inquiry-based learning in kindergarten.

Capacity
How are you feeling about your capacity to do more inquiry? What do you feel comfortable with and what do you need to learn more about?

THINQ

If you were writing this last chapter of *THINQ Kindergarten*, are these the six points you would choose to highlight? What would your list look like and why?

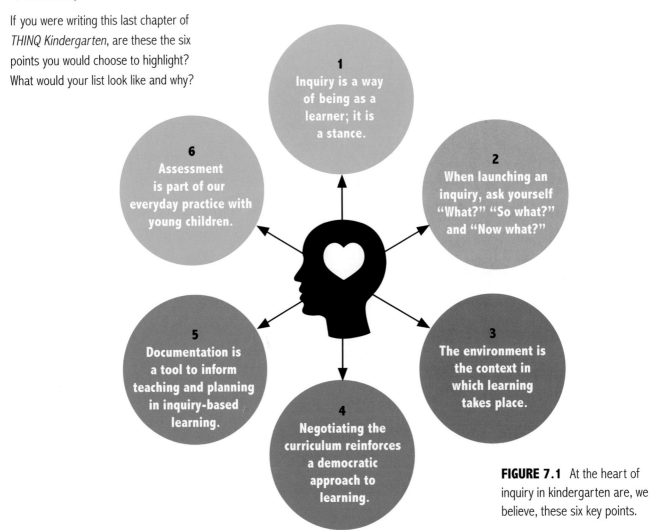

1 Inquiry is a way of being as a learner; it is a stance.

2 When launching an inquiry, ask yourself "What?" "So what?" and "Now what?"

3 The environment is the context in which learning takes place.

4 Negotiating the curriculum reinforces a democratic approach to learning.

5 Documentation is a tool to inform teaching and planning in inquiry-based learning.

6 Assessment is part of our everyday practice with young children.

FIGURE 7.1 At the heart of inquiry in kindergarten are, we believe, these six key points.

1 Inquiry is a way of being as a learner; it is a stance.

Perhaps most importantly, when embarking on inquiry, kindergarten educators need to tap into and share their own curiosity and sense of wonder. When both educators and learners open themselves up to seeing the possibility of learning in children's ideas, inquiry happens naturally. Don't wait around for a perfect inquiry question to appear or try to create one on your own. Listen with an open heart and mind, and let your learners lead the way.

Curiosity
Eagerness to learn or know something

Reflection
Ability to think about thinking

Resiliency
Capacity to keep on trying and overcome

Open-mindedness
Willingness to consider new ideas

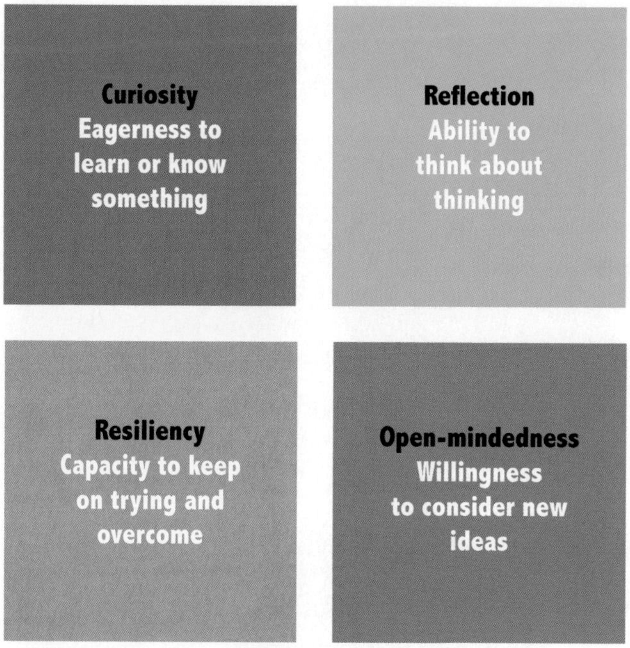

FIGURE 7.2 Curiosity, reflection, resiliency and open-mindedness are essential building blocks for creating a sustainable culture of inquiry-based learning. This applies not just to children, but educators too.

Commitment
How personally committed are you to learning alongside your kindergarten learners?

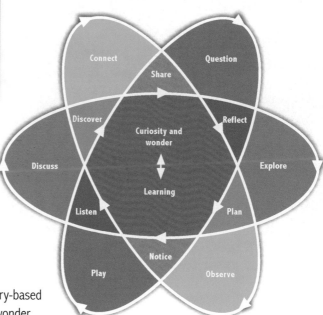

FIGURE 7.3 At the heart of all inquiry-based learning is a culture of curiosity and wonder.

2 When launching an inquiry, ask yourself "What" "So what?" and "Now what?"

We want inquiry to be meaningful and purposeful. This means that it must reflect children's ideas and connect with overall curricular expectations. Reflecting on the questions "What?" "So what?" and "Now what?" assists us in framing inquiry so it can:

- be driven by student interest and ideas,

- be purposeful in allowing learners to demonstrate their thinking in multiple ways, and

- access prior knowledge and lead to new knowledge.

Conviction
Are you convinced and hopeful that you can make inquiry both meaningful and purposeful for your learners?

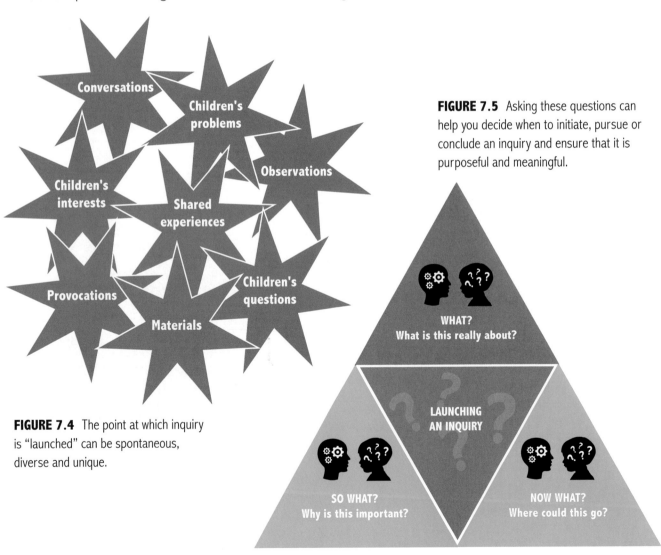

FIGURE 7.5 Asking these questions can help you decide when to initiate, pursue or conclude an inquiry and ensure that it is purposeful and meaningful.

FIGURE 7.4 The point at which inquiry is "launched" can be spontaneous, diverse and unique.

3 The environment is the context in which learning takes place.

When we reflect on the fact that kindergarten learners spend a lot of time in their classroom, we can appreciate its importance to and influence on their learning. We want and need the classroom learning environment to:

- provoke curiosity and wonder,
- create a sense of belonging, and
- communicate our beliefs about learners.

Just as importantly, when learners participate in co-constructing the spaces, materials and culture that make up a learning environment, the classroom naturally becomes a richer and more responsive place.

Context

What new ideas do you have about co-constructing a more powerful learning environment for your learners?

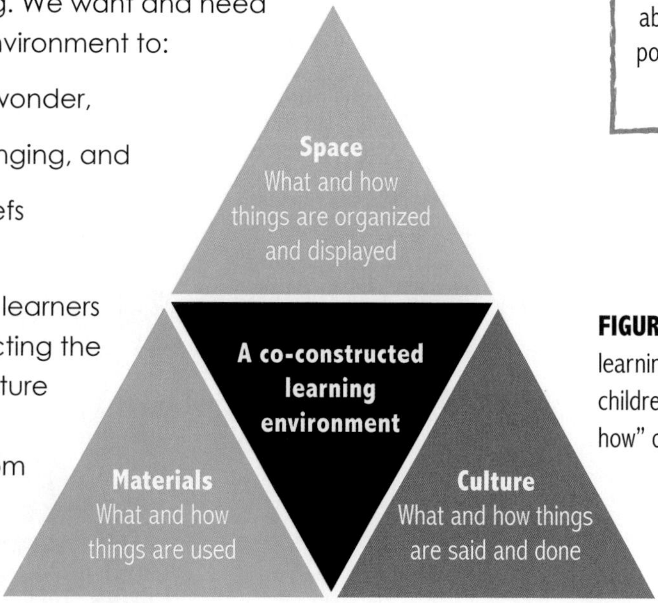

Space
What and how things are organized and displayed

A co-constructed learning environment

Materials
What and how things are used

Culture
What and how things are said and done

FIGURE 7.6 Co-constructing a learning environment means giving children a say about the "what and how" of space, materials and culture.

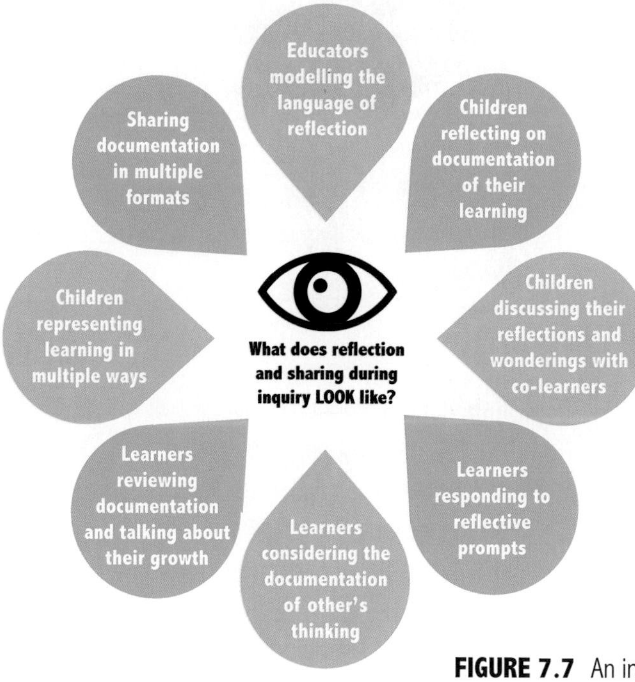

What does reflection and sharing during inquiry LOOK like?

- Educators modelling the language of reflection
- Children reflecting on documentation of their learning
- Children discussing their reflections and wonderings with co-learners
- Learners responding to reflective prompts
- Learners considering the documentation of other's thinking
- Learners reviewing documentation and talking about their growth
- Children representing learning in multiple ways
- Sharing documentation in multiple formats

What does reflection and sharing during inquiry SOUND like?

- How did you solve your problem?
- I need different stuff to figure this out.
- This doesn't make sense, I need to think about it.
- I am still wondering.
- Can you help me think about this?
- What is challenging? What will you do next?
- I wonder if there is a better way to do this?
- Why is this so hard?

FIGURE 7.7 An inquiry culture has very specific sights and sounds that educators can look and listen for.

4 Negotiating the curriculum reinforces a democratic approach to learning.

Negotiating curriculum in inquiry means children are actively involved in discussing their learning and voicing their opinions, wonderings and ideas. Educators can then use their knowledge of a kindergarten curriculum to map the skills and knowledge demonstrated and identified during inquiry onto curricular expectations. Children participating in decisions about their own learning and educators working as co-learners are the foundations of a democratic approach to learning.

Context
What does a negotiated curriculum look like in the context of your own school and classroom? How can you and your children do it better?

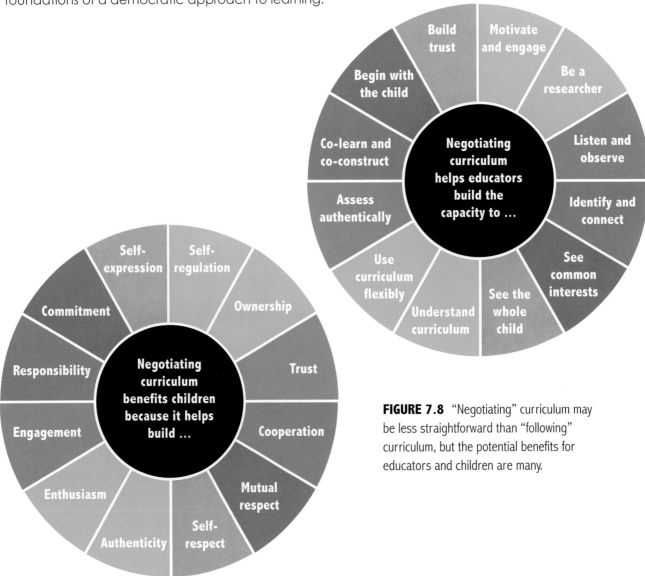

FIGURE 7.8 "Negotiating" curriculum may be less straightforward than "following" curriculum, but the potential benefits for educators and children are many.

5 Documentation is a tool to inform teaching and planning in inquiry-based learning.

The most effective way to learn about our kindergarten learners is through observation and conversation. When we observe and talk with students openly and without judgment, we can begin to see and hear what is actually happening in our classrooms. Through the interpretation of collected observations and conversations, we can analyze words and actions and theorize about the thinking and learning that is taking place. This allows us to then respond with intention and purpose. Involving learners in gathering and reflecting on documentation gives them a chance to think about their thinking too.

Confirmation
Who can you work with in your school to explore what documentation tools are most effective and efficient and how can you go about doing it?

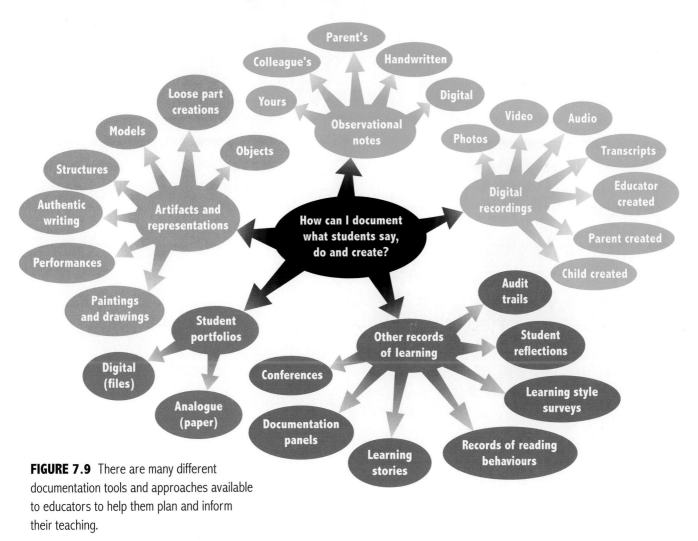

FIGURE 7.9 There are many different documentation tools and approaches available to educators to help them plan and inform their teaching.

6 Assessment is part of our everyday practice with young children.

Educators understand a child's learning by observing, talking and listening to them. If our goal is to improve learning, as it must be, then documentation and assessment for learning must be a daily and ongoing part of an educator's practice. When educators focus on using assessment to improve learning, they gain deep insights into where children are in their learning, where they need to go next and how best to get there.

Commitment
Are you committed to documenting and assessing your own assessment practice for the purpose of deepening and improving how you can identify, improve and share a child's learning?

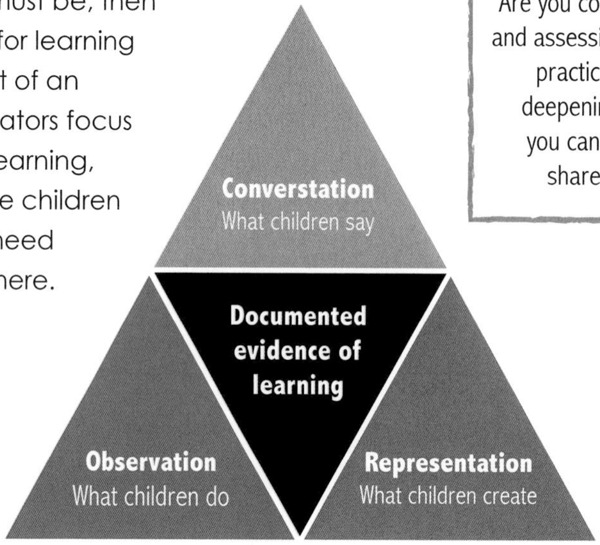

Converstation
What children say

Documented evidence of learning

Observation
What children do

Representation
What children create

FIGURE 7.10 Inquiry assessment in kindergarten means focusing on what learners are saying, doing and creating.

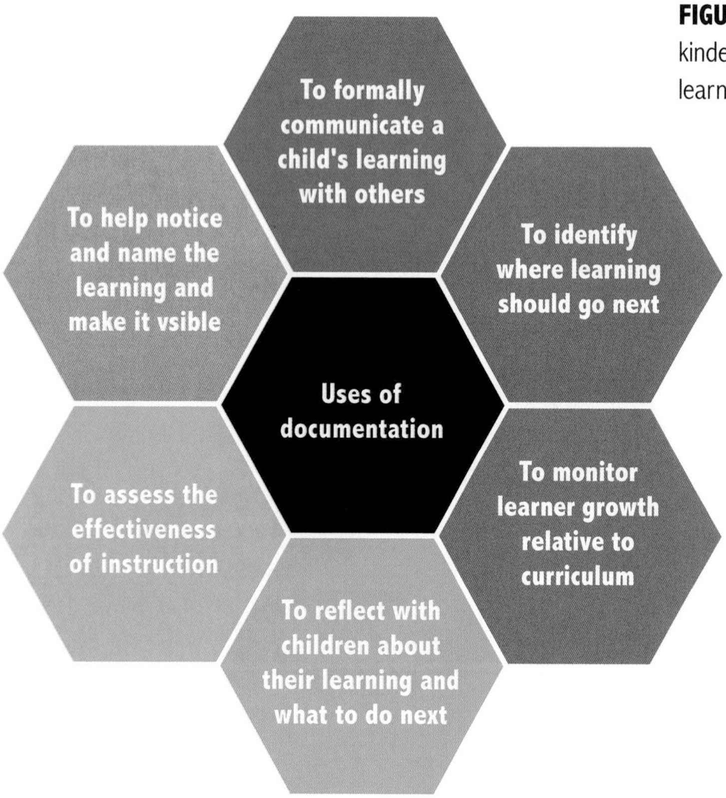

To formally communicate a child's learning with others

To help notice and name the learning and make it vsible

To identify where learning should go next

Uses of documentation

To assess the effectiveness of instruction

To monitor learner growth relative to curriculum

To reflect with children about their learning and what to do next

FIGURE 7.11 The quality and effectiveness of assessment should be measured not by how much evidence is collected, but by the degree to which it helps improve, summarize and communicate children's learning.

7.2 Final thoughts

Ultimately, an inquiry-based approach to education is about helping learners create real understandings and insights into the world in which we live, learn and work, including both natural and human-constructed environments. The questions that arise and the dilemmas we face, individually and collectively, generate the dissonance that keeps us all continuously wondering and questioning.

When we address these issues and questions within the context of an inquiry classroom, we are preparing our children to deal with the many issues and challenges they will face throughout their lives. By helping children learn "how to know" rather than just "what to know," we are getting them ready for a future we cannot begin to imagine within the context of our own time and place.

We believe that inquiry-based learning and the ability to ask and answer questions is an elemental life skill for our children. As educators, we know ourselves how exciting and motivating it can be to create inquiry schools and classrooms that engage and excite children to ask questions and delve deeper.

We want children in kindergarten to ask hard questions, think critically and engage in thoughtful reflection. In this way they can begin their journey of lifelong learning and global citizenship.

Conviction

How strong is your conviction about the imperative of starting to create lifelong inquiry thinkers and learners in kindergarten classrooms?

Traditional learning	Inquiry learning
Have to learn	Want to learn
What to know	How to know
Tell and memorize	Ask and inquire
Only one right answer	Many conclusions
Teacher directed	Learner centered
One-size-fits-all	Personalized
Passive learning	Active learning
Assess for marks	Assess for learning

FIGURE 7.12 Inquiry-based learning represents a powerful mindset for transforming teaching and learning, and creating highly capable thinkers and lifelong learners.

Reproducibles

CMEC statement on play-based learning

Learning through play is supported by science.

The benefits of play are recognized by the scientific community. There is now evidence that neural pathways in children's brains are influenced and advanced in their development through exploration, thinking skills, problem solving, and language expression that occur during play. Research also demonstrates that play-based learning leads to greater social, emotional, and academic success. Based on such evidence, ministers of education endorse a sustainable pedagogy for the future that does not separate play from learning but brings them together to promote creativity in future generations. In fact, play is considered to be so essential to healthy development that the United Nations has recognized it as a specific right for all children.

Learning through play is supported by experts.

Learning through play is supported by early years experts. Lev Vygotsky identified play as the leading source of development in terms of emotional, social, physical, language, or cognitive development. Psychologist David Elkind [states] that "play is not only our creative drive; it's a fundamental mode of learning." Such experts recognize that play and academic work are not distinct categories for young children: creating, doing, and learning are inextricably linked. When children are engaged in purposeful play, they are discovering, creating, improvising, and expanding their learning. Viewing children as active participants in their own development and learning allows educators to move beyond preconceived expectations about what children should be learning, and focus on what they are learning.

Learning through play is supported by children and parents.

Learning through play is supported by children. It is their natural response to the environment around them. When children are manipulating objects, acting out roles, or experimenting with different materials, they are engaged in learning through play. Play allows them to actively construct, challenge, and expand their own understandings through making connections to prior experiences, thereby opening the door to new learning. Intentional play-based learning enables children to investigate, ask questions, solve problems, and engage in critical thinking. Play is responsive to each child's unique learning style and capitalizes on his or her innate curiosity and creativity. Play-based learning supports growth in the language and culture of children and their families.

When children are playing, children are learning.

Given the evidence, CMEC believes in the intrinsic value and importance of play and its relationship to learning. Educators should intentionally plan and create challenging, dynamic, play-based learning opportunities. Intentional teaching is the opposite of teaching by rote or continuing with traditions simply because things have always been done that way. Intentional teaching involves educators being deliberate and purposeful in creating play-based learning environments — because when children are playing, children are learning.

Council of Ministers of Education, Canada, *Statement on play-based learning*, 2012.

Teacher inquiry readiness checklist

Check which of the following statements represents your knowledge, beliefs and understanding of inquiry learning. Use this checklist for self-reflection, for planning and sharing with colleagues, and to determine next steps in deepening your inquiry practice.

Conviction

- I believe in the main assumptions of inquiry-based learning: that learning is constructivist, child-centred, and demands critical and creative thinking.
- I am convinced by the research that advocates for taking an inquiry stance to learning in a play-based context.
- I believe that children are competent, capable, curious and full of potential.

Commitment

- I am committed to bringing more inquiry-based learning to my classroom and have reflected on not only what makes me excited, but also what makes me uncertain.
- I am connected to other committed educators who are interested in and supportive of inquiry education.

Capacity

- I understand that inquiry is an ongoing, open-ended process driven by the curiosity and wonderings of children.
- I understand what the role of a kindergarten educator is in a play-based, inquiry-driven classroom.

Context

- I have thought about my strengths as an inquiry educator and the areas in which I need to make improvements.
- I accept that inquiry learning in my classroom should be a playful, messy, recursive, iterative and non-linear experience.
- I have thought about my learners' individual readiness and disposition for inquiry and know where to start.

Confirmation

- I know what my professional goals are with respect to doing more inquiry.
- I understand how I will assess my progress, what is working, and how to improve.

The inquiry process

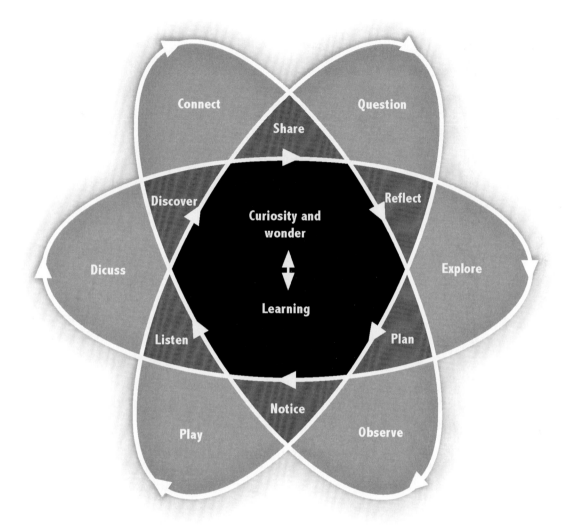

This model is intended to represent the non-linear nature of inquiry in a kindergarten classroom. Curiosity and wonder are the anchor in the middle, setting thinking in motion. The learning that follows is responsive to the individual and is iterative and flexible, with lots of looping back and reconsidering as knowledge builds. As understanding develops, more questions arise, rethinking occurs and learning becomes deeper. Communication is ongoing when educators and learners share and reflect as they question, explore and solve.

8 big ideas about inquiry-based learning in kindergarten

1

Inquiry is a way of being as a learner; it is a stance.

2

Educators must cultivate and respect the natural inquiry dispositions in every child

3

Inquiry is a non-linear process.

4

Inquiry classrooms focus on big ideas, key concepts and transferrable skills.

5

Inquiry-based learning promotes the integration of different subjects and disciplines.

6

Inquiry takes place best in purposeful, intentional, play-based environments.

7

Kindergarten learners have emerging qualities that can be intentionally strengthened through inquiry.

8

Inquiry results in children learning how to learn.

6 big ideas about wondering and questioning in kindergarten

1
Curiosity activates learning.

2
Educators must be co-learners who model their wonder and thinking with children.

3
The best questions come from learners' authentic need to know.

4
When launching an inquiry, ask yourself "What?" "So what?" and "Now what?"

5
There are many ways to provoke an inquiry.

6
Take a deep breath and let the learner's curiosity lead.

12 practices, tools and techniques to provoke inquiry in kindergarten classrooms

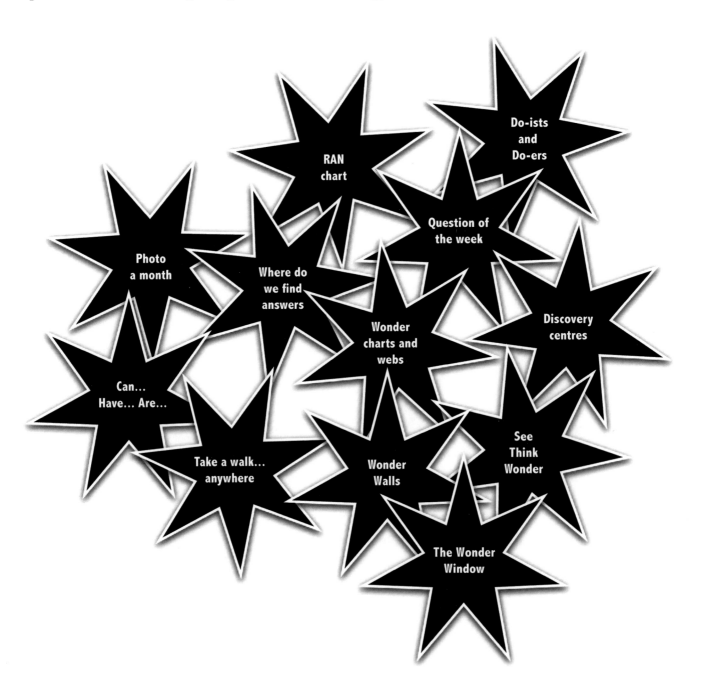

8 characteristics of robust inquiry questions

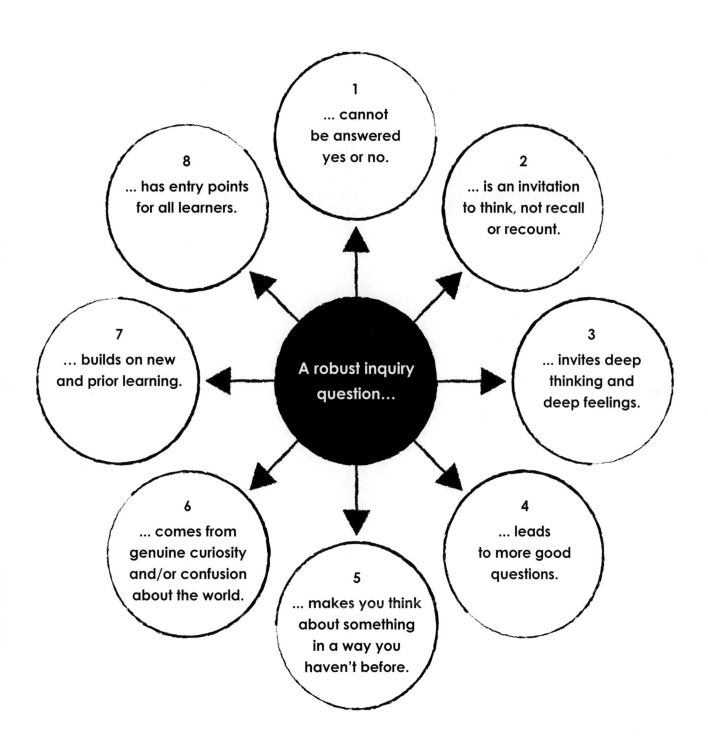

1
... cannot be answered yes or no.

2
... is an invitation to think, not recall or recount.

3
... invites deep thinking and deep feelings.

4
... leads to more good questions.

5
... makes you think about something in a way you haven't before.

6
... comes from genuine curiosity and/or confusion about the world.

7
... builds on new and prior learning.

8
... has entry points for all learners.

A robust inquiry question...

Considering educator values and the learning environment

When you examine your learning environment, use this chart as a checklist. Consider each value, then decide whether your environment supports the value or whether more consideration is need. You can then use Reproducible 3C to consider and analyze how to rearrange your environment.

Value	Value is supported	More consideration is neeed
Young children are proficient, talented and intelligent.		
Young children are capable of identifying themselves as concerned, kind, considerate, caring, thoughtful and imaginative citizens.		
Educators model and support a stance of inquiry and wonder.		
A learning environment is co-planned and co-created.		
Educators are intentional with words, actions and experiences so that children know why and what they are doing, and how to do it.		
All voices are honoured, and self-efficacy and ownership is built.		
Questioning is encouraged and supported.		
Ongoing collaboration and communication is encouraged.		
Inquiry flows throughout the day and is not subject-specific.		
Explicit teaching of skills and knowledge is done in the context of an inquiry environment.		
An inquiry-based environment supports learning that is authentic, purpose-driven and engaging.		
The structuring of time and space supports deep thinking and learning.		
Materials are chosen purposefully to support thinking and learning.		
Learners understand the intentionality of the materials.		
A co-learning relationship amongst educators, children and families supports inquiry.		
A negotiated curriculum in inquiry begins with the interests of children.		

Reflective questions about an inquiry environment

Space	Time	Resources
• Do indoor and outdoor spaces allow for differentiated instruction? • Is the space inclusive? • Has the environment been co-constructed with the children? Does it belong to them? • Has the background been neutralized to focus on student learning? • Could the space be de-cluttered? • Do the children contribute to and co-construct what is on the walls? • Is student learning visible in the form of documentation and/or student-selected pieces? • Does wall space reflect the children's interests and inquiries? • Are visual displays at student eye level? • Is there a large gathering space for whole group discussions? • Are there defined smaller gathering and quiet spaces for individuals? • Can all children move in the space with ease?	• Is our time used in a purposeful way that allows us to listen, observe and document thinking and learning? • Do we provide time and opportunity for students to make decisions and choices? • Is there time allowed for revisiting or extending an inquiry? • Does the flow of the day include a balance of teacher-initiated and child-initiated learning? • Do we ensure that there is sufficient time for children to get involved in inquiries in-depth, as well as time for them to organize their material? • Have we considered the attention span of our students so that the amount of verbal instruction suits the students' needs? • Is there time for daily classroom gatherings to share and reflect on inquiry learning?	• Do we offer a balance of open-ended materials for children to access during play? • Have we considered and chosen materials that reflect our children's real life contexts? • Have the materials, resources and equipment been organized and labeled to ensure that children can access and put them away safely and easily? (E.g., use symbols, photo labels, and word labels to indicate where things go.) • Are there a variety of materials and resources (familiar, novel, simple, complex)? • Do learners contribute to inquiry materials? • Can materials be used for multiple purposes? • Do we use knowledgeable others as a resource for our inquiries?

Rethinking the learning environment

Use this chart to make small changes in the learning environment and then reflect upon their impact.

A change or rearrangement	Values or behaviours affected	Evidence of the impact

5 big ideas about inquiry and the learning environment

1

The environment is the context in which learning takes place.

2

An inquiry environment includes the culture or tone of the classroom.

3

The use of time, space and materials needs to be purposeful.

4

An inquiry-based learning environment includes extending the classroom to the outdoors.

5

Being responsive to children's learning, growth and interests supports inquiry.

Linking observations, learning and curriculum

What did I see and hear? (Observation)	What was the learning? (Related expectations)	What was the skill? (The verb or action within the expectations)

6 big ideas about negotiating curriculum

1
Inquiry learning and kindergarten expectations are complementary.

2
A negotiated curriculum is child-initiated but educator-framed.

3
In inquiry learning, kindergarten expectations answer the question "What should be taught?"

4
Negotiating the curriculum reinforces a democratic approach to learning.

5
The negotiated curriculum starts with the child.

6
There are many advantages for the child, their family and educators with a negotiated curriculum.

A protocol for documentation

Step	Description	Collaboration

Study the documentation	**Focus: Describe the documentation**
	• Carefully study and describe the documentation.
	• Make notes:
	  • I saw …
	  • I heard …
		Review notes with colleagues, compare and contrast descriptions and observations.

Interpret the documentation	**Focus: Understand what it is telling you** • When I saw/heard … I thought … • The learning demonstrated was … • What does the documentation suggest about the child's thinking? • What are some questions we have? • What are our assumptions about the children and the learning? • What ideas and questions are children exploring? • How did my words/actions influence the experience? • Were there other influencing factors (e.g., other educators or children, environmental elements, shared learning, accommodations)? • What changes am I noticing over time and what do I do differently?	Share and discuss with colleagues. Be open to listening to all points of view and engaging in self-examination as well.
Consider implications for practice	**Focus: Apply what you learned** • What are the implications of this documentation for assessment for learning? • What are the implications of this documentation for my practice? • What further evidence of learning or information do I still need? • What types of additional documentation could provide this information? • Are students the focus of documentation and partners with me in the process? • What might be the next action for the child? • How might this information be used to plan for learning? • What does the evidence suggest to inform my pedagogical moves? • Where do we go next in the learning? • Why this learning, for this child, at this time? • What further professional learning do I need or want?	Share and discuss with colleagues. Be open to listening to all points of view and engaging in self-examination as well.

28 ways to document learning

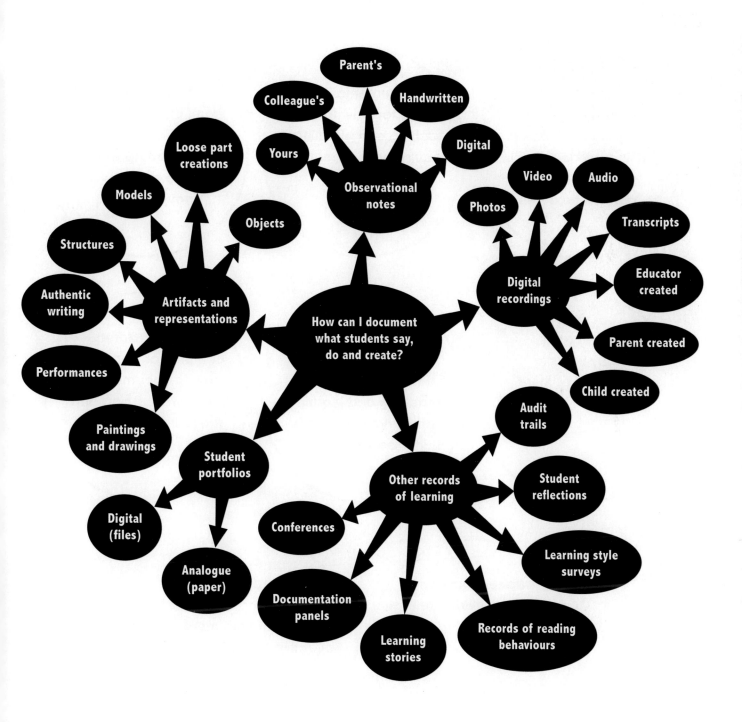

8 big ideas about documentation and inquiry in kindergarten

1
Pedagogical documentation is analyzing evidence of thinking and learning in order to develop responsive next steps.

2
Documentation is a tool to inform teaching and planning in inquiry-based learning.

3
Being aware of the stages of documentation assists us in knowing where we are and how to move forward.

4
There are as many ways to document as there are ways to learn.

5
Reflective practitioners examine the link between teaching and learning and what their role is in this relationship.

6
Young children can play an important role in documenting their own learning and the learning of others.

7
Documentation is the evidence of learning.

8
Using technology can make documentation more effective and efficient.

Purposeful planning for inquiry assessment in kindergarten

Consider the following statements in regards to how you plan for inquiry learning. You can use this checklist for self-reflection, planning and sharing with colleagues, and to determine next steps in deepening your inquiry practice.

- I understand why assessment helps children learn.

- I regularly reflect on my assessment practice and adjust it based on what has worked best to improve learning.

- Assessment for learning is a regular part of an inquiry progression and my daily conversations with students.

- I regularly notice and name the learning I see through inquiry, share it with learners and use it to plan next steps.

- I understand the current inquiry abilities of my learners and areas where growth is possible.

- I have clear learning goals that are consistent with curriculum expectations, but are shaped by my observations of and conversations with learners, what they already know and can do, and, most importantly, what they ask and wonder about.

- My learners understand our learning goals because we co-construct the criteria for success and regularly display, share and talk about them.

- My learning goals are framed in ways that allow all children to see themselves as learners and participate in learning.

- I regularly document evidence and collect artifacts of inquiry learning based on a balance of conversations, observations and representation from learners.

- I have ongoing communications with parents about inquiry in our classroom and consider how to do it in ways that accommodate the interests and needs of the families of my learners.

- I make opportunities to co-plan, co-teach and co-assess inquiry learning with colleagues.

7 big ideas about inquiry assessment in kindergarten

1

Assessment is part of our everyday practice with young children.

2

Young learners can grow and develop as inquiry thinkers.

3

Assessment for learning is fundamental for improving inquiry learning.

4

Noticing and naming the learning makes learning visible to educators and learners.

5

Learning goals help co-learners to notice and name the learning.

6

Documentation provides an authentic account of a student's learning.

7

Ongoing communication with families about learning in the inquiry classroom is vital to the home-school relationship.

Sources

Chapter 1

Early Learning for Every Child Today. Queen's Printer, 2007.

How Does Learning Happen? Ontario Pedagogy for the Early Years. The Queen's Printer, 2014.

Lewin-Benham, Ann. *Twelve Best Practices for Early Childhood Education.* Teachers College Press, 2011.

Kuhlithau, Carol C., Maniotes, Leslie K., and Ann K. Caspari. *Guided Inquiry: Learning in the 21st Century.* Libraries Unlimited, 2007.

Natural Curiosity: A Resource for Teachers. The Lab School at the Institute of Child Study. Maracle Press, 2011.

Richart, Ron, Church, Mark and Karin Morrison. *Making Thinking Visible: How to Promote Engagement, Understanding and Independence for all Learners.* Jossey-Bass, 2011.

Rinaldi, Carla. *The Relationship Between Documentation and Assessment.* Innovations in Early Education, 2004.

Timperley, Helen, Kaser, Linda and Judy Halbert. *A framework for transforming learning in schools: Innovation and the spiral of inquiry.* Centre for Strategic Education, Seminar Series Paper No. 234 (2014, April).

Wien, Carol Anne. *Emergent Curriculum in the Primary Classroom: Interpreting the Reggio Emilia Approach in Schools.* Teachers College Press, 2008.

Chapter 2

Ciccone, Tisiana. "So What?" Extraordinary Classroom. Written May 20, 2016. https://reggiokids.blogspot.ca/2016/05/so-what.html

Stead, Tony. *Reality Checks: Teaching Reading Comprehension with Nonfiction, K–5.* Stenhouse Publishers, 2005.

All images courtesy of the authors.

Chapter 3

Hare, Rebecca Louise and Dr. Robert Dillon. *The Space: A Guide for Educators.* EdTech Team Press, 2016.

The Lab School at the Institute of Child Study. *Natural Curiosity: A Resource for Teachers.* Maracle Press, 2011.

Lewin-Benham, Ann. *Twelve Best Practices for Early Childhood Education.* Teachers College Press, 2011.

Maynard, Trisha and Jane Waters. "Learning in the outdoor environment: a missed opportunity?" *Early Years*, 27:3, 255–265 (2007).

Ontario Ministry of Education. *Capacity Building Series*, "Student Voice: Transforming Relationships." September 2013.

The Outdoor Classroom Project. http://outdoorclassroomproject.org/

All images courtesy of the authors.

Chapter 4

All images courtesy of the authors.

Chapter 5

Helm, Judy Harris, Beneke, Sallee and Kathy Steinheimer. *Windows on Learning.* New York, NY: Teachers College Press, 2007.

Krechevsky, Mara, Mardell, Ben, Rivard, Melissa and Daniel Wilson, *Visible Learners: Promoting Reggio-Inspired Approaches in All Schools.* Jossey-Bass, 2013.

Lewin-Benham, Ann. *Twelve Best Practices for Early Childhood Education.* Teachers College Press, 2011.

Ontario Ministry of Education. *Capacity Building Series*, "Pedagogical Documentation" 2012.

Project Zero and Reggio Children. *Making Learning Visible: Children as Individual and Group Learners.* Reggio Children, 2001.

Rinaldi, Carla. "The Pedagogy of Listening: The Listening Perspective from Reggio Emilia." *The Hundred Languages of Children: The Reggio Approach in Transformation, 3rd Edition.* Edwards, Badini and Forman, 2012.

Seitz, Hilary. "The Power of Documentation in the Early Childhood Classroom." *Young Children.* March 2008.

All images courtesy of the authors.

Chapter 6

Rinaldi, Carla. *The Relationship Between Documentation and Assessment.* Innovations in Early Education, 2004.

All images courtesy of the authors.

Bibliography

Books

Barrel, John. *Why Are School Buses Always Yellow? Teaching for Inquiry PreK–5*. Corwin Press, 2008.

Carr, Margaret. *Assessment in Early Childhood Settings*. Sage, 2001.

Carr, Margaret and Wendy Lee. *Learning Stories*. Sage, 2012.

Curtis, Deb and Margie Carter. *Designs for Living and Learning: Transforming Early Childhood Environments, 2nd Edition*. Redleaf Press, 2015.

Eden, Susanne and Janet Millar Grant. *Primarily Play: Engaging Learners Through Play*. Elementary Teachers' Federation of Ontario, 2011.

Edwards, Carolyn, Gandini, Lella and George Forman, ed. *The Hundred Languages of Children, Third Edition*. Santa Barbara, California. Praeger, 2012.

Fraser, Susan. *Authentic Childhood: Experiencing Reggio Emilia in the Classroom Third Edition*. Toronto: Nelson Education Ltd., 2006.

Gray, Peter. *The Value of Play I: The Definition of Play Gives Insights*. Retrieved from https://www.psychologytoday.com/blog/freedom-learn/200811/the-value-play-i-the-definition-play-gives-insights, 2008.

Hare, Rebecca Louise and Dr. Robert Dillon. *The Space: A Guide for Educators*. EdTech Team Press, 2016.

Hattie, John. *What Works Best in Education: The Politics of Collaborative Expertise*. Pearson, 2015.

Hattie, John. *What Works Best in Education: The Politics of Distraction*. Pearson, 2015.

Heard, Georgia and McDonough, Jennifer. *A Place for Wonder: Reading and Writing Nonfiction in the Primary Grades*. Stenhouse Publishers, 2009.

Helm, Judy Harris, Beneke, Sallee and Kathy Steinheimer. *Windows on Learning*. New York, NY: Teachers College Press, 2007.

Helm, Judy Harris and Katz, Lillian. *Young Investigators: The Project Approach in the Early Years*. Teachers College Press, 2011.

Heritage, Margaret. *Formative Assessment and Next-Generation Assessment Systems: Are We Losing an Opportunity?* Los Angeles: National Center for Research on Evaluation, Standards and Student Testing, 2010.

Heritage, Margaret. *Formative Assessment in Practice*. Cambridge, Massachusetts: Harvard Education Press, 2013.

Hill, Peter and Michael Barber. *Preparing for a Renaissance in Assessment*. Pearson, 2014.

Johnston, Peter H. *Choice Words: How Our Language Affects Children's Learning*. Stenhouse Publishers, 2004.

Krechevsky, Mara, Mardell, Ben, Rivard, Melissa and Daniel Wilson, *Visible Learners- Promoting Reggio-Inspired Approaches in All Schools*. San Francisco, CA: Jossey-Bass, 2013.

Lester, Stuart and Wendy Russell. *Children's right to play: An examination of the importance of play in the lives of children worldwide*. Bernard van Leer Foundation, The Hague, The Netherlands: December 2010.

Lewin-Benham, Ann. *Twelve Best Practices for Early Childhood Education*. Teachers College Press, 2011.

Manguel, Alberto. *Curiosity*. Yale University Press, 2015.

McTigue, Jay and Grant Wiggins. *Essential Questions: Opening doors to student understanding*. Association for Supervision and Curriculum Development, 2013.

Miller, Edward and Joan Almon. *Crisis in the Kindergarten: Why Children Need to Play in School*. College Park, MD: Alliance for Childhood, 2009.

Morgan, Norah and Saxton, Juliana, *Asking Better Questions, 2nd Edition*. Pembroke Publishers, 2006.

Moss, Connie M. and Susan Brookhart. *Advancing Formative Assessment in Every Classroom*. Alexandria, Virginia: ASCD, 2009.

Richart, Ron, Church, Mark and Morrison, Karin. *Making Thinking Visible: How to Promote Engagement, Understanding and Independence for all Learners*. Jossey-Bass Publishers, 2011.

Ontario Ministry of Education, *The Kindergarten Program 2016*. Queen's Printer for Ontario, 2016.

Schein, Edgar H. *Humble Inquiry*. San Francisco, CA: Barrett-Koehler Publishers, Inc., 2013.

Stacey, Susan. *Pedagogical Documentation in Early Childhood: Sharing Children's Learning and Teacher's Thinking*. Redleaf Press, 2015.

The Lab School at the Institute of Child Study. *Natural Curiosity: A Resource for Teachers*. Maracle Press, 2011.

Watt, Jennifer and Jill Colyer. *IQ: A Practical Guide to Inquiry-Based Learning*. Toronto: Oxford University Press, 2014.

Wiliam, Dylan. *Embedded Formative Assessment*. Bloomington, IN: Solution Tree Press, 2011.

Wein, Carol Anne. *The Power of Emergent Curriculum: Stories from Early Childhood Settings*. National Association for the Education of Young Children, 2014.

White, Rachel E. *The Power of Play: A Research Summary on Play and Learning*. Minnesota Children's Museum, 2012.

Wurm, Julianne P. *Working in the Reggio Way: A Beginner's Guide for American Teachers*. Redleaf Press, 2005.

Articles

Boud, David. "Sustainable Assessment: rethinking assessment for the learning society." *Studies in Continuing Education, Vol. 22, No.2, 2000.*

Carr, Margaret. "Young children reflecting on their learning: teachers' conversation strategies." *Early Years: An International Journal of Research and Development, 31:3, pp. 257–270, September 2011.*

Chappuis, Stephen, Chappuis, Jan and Rick Stiggins, "The Quest for Quality."

Educational Leadership, November 2009.

Davies, Anne, Busick, Kathy, Herbst, Sandra and Ann Sherman. "System Leaders using assessment for learning as both the change and the change process: developing theory from practice." *The Curriculum Journal.* October 2014.

Druckor, Brent. "Formative Assessment in Seven Good Moves", *Educational Leadership,* March 2014.

Dunphy, Elizabeth. "Assessing early learning through formative assessment: key issues and considerations." *Irish Educational Studies,* September 2010.

Edelstein, Wolfgang. "Education for Democracy: reasons and strategies." *European Journal of Education, Vol. 46, No. 1, 2011.*

Edwards, Carol Pope and Gandini, Lella. "Teacher Research in Reggio Emilia: Essence of a Dynamic and Evolving Role." *Voices of Practitioners,* Winter 2015.

Fielding, Michael. "Beyond Student Voice: Patterns of Partnership and the Demands of Deep Democracy." *Revista de Educacion, 359, Septiembre-diciembre, 2012 pp 45–65.*

Hamlin, Maria and Debora B. Wisneski. "Supporting the Scientific Thinking and Inquiry of Toddlers and Preschoolers through Play." *Young Children,* May 2012.

Harste, Jerome. "What Education as Inquiry Is and Isn't." *Critiquing Whole Language and Classroom Inquiry,* NCTE, 2001.

Heritage, Margaret. "Formative Assessment: What Do Teachers Need to Know and Do?" *Phi Delta Kappan, Vol. 89, No. 02. Pp. 140–145.* October 2007.

Hunter, Thelma and Glenda Walsh. "From policy to practice?: the reality of play in primary school classes in northern Ireland." *International Journal of Early Years Education. Vol. 22. No. 1 pp. 19–36. 2014.*

Ogu, Uchenna and Suzie Reynard Schmidt. "Investigating Rocks and Sand: Addressing Multiple Learning Styles through an Inquiry-Based Approach." *Beyond the Journal – Young Children on the Web,* March 2009.

Jones, Elizabeth. "The Emergence of Emergent Curriculum." *Young Children,* March 2012.

Maynard, Trish and Jane Waters. "Learning in the Outdoor Environment: A missed opportunity?" *Early Years 27:3, 255–265,* September 2007.

McDonald, Margaret. "Toward formative assessment: The use of pedagogical documentation in early elementary classrooms." *Early Childhood Research Quarterly, 22, p. 232–242, 2007.*

Mistrett, Sue and Bickart, Toni. "Child's Play: The Best Way to Learn." *MEE- May–June 2009 www.middleeasterneducator.com*

Moss, Peter and Gunilla Dahlberg. "Beyond Quality in Early Childhood Education and Care – Languages of Evaluation." *New Zealand Journal of Teachers' Work, Volume 5, Issue 1, 03-12, 2008.*

Ontario Ministry of Education. Think Feel Act: Lessons from Research about Young Children, Queens Printer for Ontario, 2013.

Ontario Ministry of Education Capacity Building Series: Inquiry Based Learning, 2013.

Ontario Ministry of Education Capacity Building Series: The Third Teacher, 2012.

Ontario Ministry of Education Capacity Building Series: Getting Started with Student Inquiry, 2011.

Ontario Ministry of Education Capacity Building Series: Pedagogical Documentation, 2012.

Ontario Ministry of Education Capacity Building Series: Asking Effective Questions, 2011.

Ontario Ministry of Education Capacity Building Series: Student Voice, Transforming Relationships, 2013.

Ontario Ministry of Education: K–2 Connections Digital Paper. https://kto2connections.wordpress.com/

Samuelsson, Ingrid Pramling and Maj Asplund Carlsson. "The Playing Learning Child: Towards a pedagogy of early childhood." *Scandinavian Journal of Educational Research, Volume 52, No 6, pp. 623–641,* December 2008.

Samuelsson, Ingrid Pramling and Niklas Pramling. "Children's perspectives as 'touch downs' in time: assessing and developing children's understanding simultaneously." *Early Child Development and Care. Vol. 179, No. 2, pp. 205–2016,* February 2009.

Shepard, Lorrie A. "The Challenges of Assessing Young Children Appropriately." *Phi Delta Kappan magazine,* November 1994.

Swaffield, Sue. "Getting to the heart of authentic Assessment for Learning." *Assessment in Education: Principles, Policy and Practice.* November 2011.

Temperley, Helen, Kaser, Linda, and Judy Halbert. "A framework for transforming learning in schools: Innovation and the spiral of inquiry." *Center for Strategic Education,* 2014.

Turner, Terri and Daniel Gray Wilson. "Reflections on Documentation: A Discussion with Thought Leaders from Reggio Emilia." *Theory into Practice, 49:5–13,* 2010.

Wien, Carol Anne. "Emergent Curriculum." *Connections,* Vol 10.1, April 2006.

Wien, Carol Anne, Jacobs, Brenda and Ellen Brown. "Emergent Curriculum and the Tension Between Relationship and Assessment." *Contemporary Perspectives on Research in Assessment and Evaluation in Early Childhood education, pp. 93–114,* 2015.

Wien, Carol Anne, Guyevskey, Victoria and Berfoussis Noula, "Learning to Document in Reggio-inspired Education." *Early Childhood Research and Practice, Vol 13, No 2,* 2011.

Wiliam, Dylan. "The Right Questions, The Right Way." *Educational Leadership,* March 2014.

"Why Consider Outdoor Classrooms." Classrooms in Nature. http://classroominnature.weebly.com/why-consider-outdoor-classrooms.html

Index